DREAMING ON PURPOSE

Dreaming
ON PURPOSE

A Manifesto for Black Women on
Taking the Leap, Building Your Dreams
& Being Your Own Boss

ARIANE HUNTER

Library of Congress Control Number: 2023919603
Paperback ISBN: 978-1-954676-72-5
eBook ISBN: 978-1-954676-73-2

Although this publication is designed to provide accurate information about the subject matter, the publisher and the author assume no responsibility for any errors, inaccuracies, omissions, or inconsistencies herein. This publication is intended as a resource, however, it is not intended as a replacement for direct and personalized professional services.

Editors: Deborah Froese, Mary Ward Menke
Cover and Interior Design: Emma Elzinga
Author Photo: Michelle Magdalena

Printed in the United States of America

First Edition

3 West Garden Street, Ste. 718
Pensacola, FL 32502
www.indigoriverpublishing.com

Ordering Information:

Quantity sales: Special discounts are available on quantity purchases by corporations, associations, and others. For details, contact the publisher at the address above.

Orders by US trade bookstores and wholesalers: Please contact the publisher at the address above.

With Indigo River Publishing, you can always expect great books, strong voices, and meaningful messages. Most importantly, you'll always find . . . *words worth reading.*

CONTENTS

Foreword IX

Preface XIII

1 When the J-O-B becomes WTF 1
    Dreaming Ourselves Free 6
    A Rude Awakening. 8
    Purpose 14
    The Shake-Up 18
    The New Truth about Dreams 20
    Purpose to Practice 23

2 Taking the Leap 27
    When We Take the Leap 29
    The Changing Landscape 34
    The First Three Years of Your Business 35
    A Dream Without a Plan is Just a Wish. 36
    Purpose to Practice 43

3 F*ck Fear 45
    Narratives of Fear 46
    You Can't Outrun Fear. 50
    Fear and Confidence 52
    The Confidence Barriers We Can't See 56
    When You Don't Feel Qualified 60
    Navigating Fear in Four Ways. 61
    Purpose to Practice 62

4 Mind Over Money 63

   Early Money Memories 67

   Money Mindset. 70

   The Money Practice that Changed My Life. 71

   Melanin and Money 74

   Purpose to Practice 79

5 Build Your Brand, Build a Legacy .81

   What is a Brand?. 83

   Knowing Your Why 85

   Our Cultural Upbringing is an Asset. 88

   Your Brand is Your Legacy 91

   Doing Work that You Believe In. 94

   Start With Your Mission Statement 96

   Envision Your Funeral 98

   Determining Your Earthly Assignment. 98

   Purpose to Practice 99

6 This is How We Market 101

   Seen and Not Heard. 102

   Stop Hiding 104

   Introverts Make the Best Marketers. 105

   Marketing through Storytelling 109

   Know Your Audience. 110

   Your Message. 111

   Choose Your Stage (Marketing Channel) 112

   Make it Measurable 114

   Purpose to Practice 115

7 Mentorship and Building Up Your Army of Angels 117

   Our Earliest Mentors 120

   Mentoring and Being Mentored. 122

   Cultivating a Mentoring Relationship 128

   Finding and Working with A Mentor 129

Building Mentor Relationships. 130
Put Away the Strong, Independent Black Woman Narrative . . 131
Networking and Building Your Army of Angels 133
The Power of Many. 134
Undoing Networking Nerves 135
What Do You Do? Is Canceled 137
Purpose to Practice 140

8 Rest Culture 141
Lazy or Luxury 142
Team No Sleep 143
The Impact of Driving Too Hard 144
The Time We All Stayed Home. 145
Go Lay Down 146
Not Returning to Normal 148
Tips to Rest & Recover. 149
Purpose to Practice 150

9 Catching the Spirit 151
Healing from Harm 153
Embracing the Woo 154
The Mind-Spirit Connection 159
Accessing Your Intuition 161
The Intersection of Business and Spirituality 163
Creating Your Own Spiritual Practice. 166
Purpose to Practice 167

10 The Path Forward **169**
Purpose to Practice 172

About the Author 175

Acknowledgments. 177

FOREWORD

AFTER TAKING THE LEAP FROM a seventeen-year career at the US Chamber of Commerce and five years of entrepreneurship, I met Ariane. It was the end of 2017 during an event at the New York Society for Ethical Culture. I had been invited to speak for The Academi of Life, a social enterprise and place of higher learning founded by leader in the wellness space and serial entrepreneur, Shirley Moulton. It offers participants a fascinating look at human nature through discussions about big questions around love, family, work, money, and living in a fast paced world.

At the time, I was just starting my career as a speaker. Although I was truly honored that Shirley had provided me with an opportunity to participate, my confidence level was not the best; I often compared myself to other more experienced speakers. That day, I spoke about self-mastery, drawing from my own experience as an entrepreneur.

Right after I finished speaking, Ariane came up and introduced herself. She told me that she had enjoyed the talk and the message. It made me feel so good and happy; it was just the boost I needed for that day! I liked Ariane from the first minute, and immediately noticed something special about her. She was a young, driven individual with a gentle voice and strong presence.

Several months later, Ariane sent an email inviting me to lunch. She wanted to discuss the possibility of me mentoring her. Her determination was clear from my perspective, and I knew that she had the potential to go far.

Ariane was the perfect mentee. She was trusting and willing to learn. Each day, she became more of the person she was meant to be. We met each week both virtually and in person. Sometimes I assigned homework to test her. She would sometimes ask, "What is this for?"

I'd laugh and say, "Do it, and you will see for yourself."

Today I am very happy that we are now close friends. Sisters.

One thing I admire about Ariane is her commitment to empowering those around her, particularly when it comes to thriving in our career. She carries out that commitment tirelessly. She is a woman of faith, and she always looks to her inner compass to show her the way. From the last five years of knowing Ariane, I have witnessed her continuously improve her craft and step fully into her power as a business leader. She goes step by step in fulfilling her vision, and when she encounters any adversity, she does not let it stop her. She walks with clear truth and purpose as she knows the stakes are high as a Black woman in business. This book illustrates her generosity, her willingness to share her wisdom and her path with you.

When I finished reading *Dreaming on Purpose*, I felt so much gratitude and pride! The book is filled with Ariane's personality. Her charm and witty voice comes across with humor and practicality. She has a mission, and she doesn't play around! She wants to help more Black women succeed as entrepreneurs and take charge of our own destinies. She knows that her calling in life is to push back on systemic inequities, reconnect with our dreams as Black women, so we can become the best version of ourselves.

I am honored to write the foreword for her first book (she will write more for sure!) because it's the kind of book that I want in my library to read many times over.

It's time for Black women to love ourselves even deeper, reclaim our time, and build the ladder so that we and our sisters can climb to the place we deserve to be in society. This is the moment to step into becoming powerful creators of our dream lives.

My dear reader, when you trust in yourself and listen to your heart, the world will open up to you. Ariane is living proof of this! Follow the guidance that's in this book and you will find yourself on a very deep and rewarding path!

Enjoy the journey!

Bisila Bokoko, Global Leadership Advisor, Speaker & CEO at BBES

November 2022

Madrid, Spain

PREFACE

ON'T LET THE NICE, SMILEY woman with the big hair on the cover of this book talking about living your dreams fool you. I'm about to shake up some shit in your career that you might not be ready for. But don't worry; we're gonna proceed with love. You see, my mission is to get you to see that your days of staying in that soul-sucking job without making the money you are worth and sacrificing your needs instead of claiming those dreams inside of you—those days are over. I want to invite you into a new conversation about taking leaps and radically pushing back on the social paradigms and generational ideas about work and livelihood that literally have you surviving instead of thriving. Together, we're going to unpack toxic systems that we live in every day that would rather see us erased, silenced, and passed over. I see the pain that comes from silencing our voices. It keeps us hidden instead of taking up space. We've tolerated "good enough" for far too long. I want better for us. I believe that entrepreneurship is the way out and the way through; it's how we get free.

From a young age, I was eager to learn about business and commerce. In high school, I took a few introduction to business classes. One was a typing class. I picked up the skill pretty quickly. By the time I got to college, I realized that the ability to type fast was rare. While I could sail through a twenty- to thirty-page assignment with ease, other students sometimes spent hours on the keyboard struggling to type. I think we all can relate to the stress and anxiety of trying to complete a lengthy assignment to hand in the next day.

Right away I recognized three things: the problem, the solution that was quite literally at my fingertips, and how a college student with looming tuition bills could make some extra cash.

An entrepreneur was born.

I made a decent amount of money that semester by charging a dollar per page to students who needed a quick and accurate typist. College seniors hired me to type out thesis papers and essays. Sometimes I even typed out resumes since getting a job after college was top of mind for them. I remember making fifty bucks for just one hour of work! That was a whole lot of money for me back then. I probably could have charged a lot more for my services, but hey, my clients were broke college students too. To me, business was good. I had a niche and a marketable skill that made me money.

That first taste of entrepreneurship had me hooked. Making money by helping people gave me confidence and instilled a sense of agency over my life. I learned to make decisions to better myself and others. While I always imagined myself as some high-powered business executive, I never imagined I would one day actually go into business for myself. But as a Black woman who has tried succeeding as one of the *only* persons of color in most white corporate settings, my path towards entrepreneurship was inevitable.

The truth is most office workplaces were not designed for us to advance but for us to remain unseen and our work undervalued. If we can't find fulfillment and appreciation as an employee, we're going to find it elsewhere, and most times that means starting our own thing.

Besides my side hustle as a college student, most folks don't know that my first real foray into entrepreneurship was actually as a freelance photographer. I freelanced for two years as a wedding and portrait photographer which taught me how to get clients and earn money from my creative passions. I learned as a business owner that it was my vision and values that drove my success more than the quality of my pictures. But don't get it twisted: I could damn sure take some beautiful photos in my day.

After a good run, I closed up my photography business. Several months later, a serendipitous encounter with a former photo client led me to pursue a career in coaching and professional development. This client became a friend and knew my story of leaving corporate to start my dreams. She asked if I would consider becoming a coach and helping people find their career direction. You know when you hear an idea and it immediately feels like a "hell yes"? That's exactly how it felt in my belly, an instant excitement at the thought of helping people do what brings them joy. I got my coaching certification and subsequently became the founder of Project She Went for Her Dreams, a coaching and consultancy firm mission was to empower and advance women within their careers. I started a business in one of the most saturated, highly competitive markets: New York City. For over a decade, I've had the honor of coaching and mentoring hundreds of the most brilliant, creative minds to own their career path.

Sometimes entrepreneurship is like a tattoo; you can't just stop at one. In 2019, I launched a second company, My Mentors Circle, a mentor-matching program for Black women founders. Through this circle, members receive and gain access to seasoned mentors who look like them and become supportive partners.

Like many Black women who start businesses, I was frustrated by my own personal experience which lacked access to mentors during the early stages of my entrepreneurial journey. I wanted to work with someone who looked like me, someone I could relate to, someone who had the kind of success that I envisioned for myself. I was tired of seeing other women entrepreneurs of color claw their way through the process to claim their rightful place at the table—all without having access to the same mentoring opportunities, resources, or communities that were available to other groups.

Throughout the years, I've spoken on stages and been interviewed by the media. I've been in rooms with some of the most powerful women in business whose combined net worth is in the millions, many times elbowing my way through to get a fair shot and create my own path. At times, I've made multiple five figures in just one month, and at other times, I've had just two figures in my business bank account. Sometimes I still wonder how I got to where I am today, but like my mother would say, when I lock in on what I want, I'm like a dog with a bone.

When it comes to entrepreneurship, I've experienced the highs and the lows. I've seen it all, which is why being a business owner doesn't scare me. I faced what most people are afraid of and came out stronger on the other side. While it wasn't easy, with the help of my greatest supporters, I never gave up.

Growing up, it was rare to see Black people—let alone Black women—in successful, thriving businesses. I didn't learn about Madame C. J. Walker, the first Black woman millionaire, until I was in my thirties. Black heroes, trailblazers, Black Wall Street, and stories from history were not taught in classrooms. Through the early years of my business and corporate career, just about all the books I saw in bookstores were mainly authored by white men and women.

For hundreds of years, Black women weren't allowed to own businesses much less anything else. We were considered property in the 1800s. History shows us that the souls and bodies of Black women were not even ours to own. Instead, they belonged to a cruel and wicked system that devalued our existence. Women weren't permitted to own land or possess property until 1848 when the Married Woman's Property Act was passed in New York. Under this law, women were allowed to conduct business on their own and have ownership of gifts they received, including land. While this signified progress for *women's* rights, it did not include *Black* women or Black people for that matter, as enslavement was still practiced in the US at that time.

If people of color were not granted rights to property or economic progress in any meaningful way for hundreds of years, is it any wonder why we still see gaps in Black wealth generation and ownership today? Black women continue to be paid less than non-Black individuals. Black women founders still receive less in venture capital funding year over year.

Before the COVID-19 pandemic, Black women were the fastest

growing segment of entrepreneurs, but the pandemic has only widened an already inequitable playing field. The businesses of those women are treading water just to stay afloat. The pandemic shuttered 41 percent of Black-owned businesses, compared to just 17 percent of white-owned businesses.[1]

The sobering reality is this: we still have a long way to go to achieve racial and gender equity in this country. The flip side is that we are seeing a change in how we work. The face of entrepreneurship is shifting from Silicon Valley tech bros who send themselves to the moon to Black and brown women like Melissa Butler, CEO and founder of The Lip Bar; Robyn Rihanna Fenty and Lisa Price of Carol's Daughter; Hannah Diop, creator and cofounder of Sienna Naturals hair care line; Tonya Rapley, financial guru and founder of My Fab Finance; Minda Harts, founder of The Memo; and trailblazer Karen Mitchell of True Indian Hair based in my hometown of New York City.

Look at us. We're really out here doing our thing! Seriously, I could go on and on with this list of amazing Black women entrepreneurs, but my point is this: if it's possible for these extraordinary ladies to succeed, it is sure as hell possible for you!

When you are making, creating, and working at something you care about, AND getting PAID for it, you can: say *eff it* to that soul-sucking job, make the money you want to make, and have the freedom to live your life on your own terms. Entrepreneurship can greatly increase your earning power, leading you to more equitable economic opportunities. Entrepreneurship can lead you to build generational wealth. Hell, through entrepreneurship, you can even say *buh bye* to that lame partner who says they love you but always finds a way to hurt you. Don't get them back by going to the club, get them back by earning that paper. Like Beyonce said, it's the best revenge.

---

1   Ruth Umoh, "Black Women Were Among The Fastest-Growing Entrepreneurs— Then Covid Arrived," *Forbes*, accessed June 5, 2022, https://www.forbes.com/sites/ ruthumoh/2020/10/26/black-women-were-among-the-fastest-growing-entrepre- neurs-then-covid-arrived/?sh=35e2b9956e01.

If you're thinking about taking the leap and starting your own business, the only two words you'll ever need to hear are these: *Start Now!*

In my opinion, choosing to become an entrepreneur is one of the most thrilling and rewarding decisions you can make in your career. But first, a little disclaimer: It's also the most daunting, scariest things one can do. It will keep you up at night, it will be all you ever talk about, and your permanent address as a new entrepreneur will be 111 Uncertainty Lane for the rest of your days.

Becoming an entrepreneur will also bring up all of your emotional stuff—all the inner work you need to heal and undo. You'll wonder why you're not as far along as other people are as the doom of self comparison sets in. You think you suck at sales, so you'll avoid activities that will bring you client sales in your own business. Oh, and all of your money blocks and beliefs you learned about money will come to the surface. Don't know what your money blocks are? Don't worry, they will become clear as day as you try to come up with pricing to charge clients or develop a pesky habit of procrastinating when it comes to sending out your invoice.

Entrepreneurship will teach you so much through the process of moving through your doubts and fears so that you can discover what you are capable of. And you will get to build something you are truly proud of, something that literally has the power to change the world.

Sounds too lofty, you might say. Well, this might not be the book for you. And that's okay. This book is for dreamers, doers, change makers, risk takers, bold thinkers, and those who refuse to tolerate the status quo.

The book you're holding in your hands right now is a culmination of a business I dreamed up ten years ago and dared to go after. It results from a decade of the ups and downs associated with starting a business: tough lessons learned, hard won successes, mistakes to avoid, and learning how to take big leaps in the direction of your dreams. I wrote this book to help all Black women succeed in business. Whether you're a side hustler or in the early stages of building out your business, this book will guide you through it all. But because I believe entrepreneurship is one of the most transformative journeys you'll undergo personally, this book also offers medicine for the soul when the entrepreneurial waters gets rocky. In the following pages you'll peel back the layers and take a deeper dive into self-acceptance, learn to lead, and trust in yourself.

I am writing the book I wanted to read when I started out as an entrepreneur. I hope you will see yourself reflected in the pages ahead. Use what you discover to carve your own path. I don't have all the answers, but I am honored that you are here and have chosen this book to aid your journey.

I can't promise that building your dreams will be easy, but I guarantee it is absolutely worth going for. If you're ready to put aside your fears, take the leap, and dream on purpose, pull up a seat, Sis.

Let's do this.

Chapter 1

WHEN THE J-O-B
BECOMES WTF

A T THE END OF YOUR life, what do you want to be able to say about the life you led and the work you did?

That's right, we're starting off with the hard questions. Whenever I ask people this, I am usually met with blank stares. Interestingly, when I mention that I make a living by helping people find the answers to this question, those same faces light up. It's as if something within them has been switched on for the first time. A shift away from their busy, rational thinking minds to one of possibility, hope, and expansion takes place as they consider how to respond.

I've always been fascinated by the way people choose career paths. How does one decide to become a doctor? A lawyer? An accountant? I've found that we often fall into a profession accidentally and not of our actual choosing. Usually this happens when someone, most times our parents, pushed us in that direction simply because it seemed logical. If you grew up with immigrant parents, you especially know this all too well. An example of this could be following Dad's advice to become a lawyer or go into finance because it's stable and lucrative. "People will always need doctors," you might hear your mom say. Initially, it may seem logical and a surefire way to please our parents and make them proud, but it can become problematic if you don't truly love the world of medicine.

I always loved school. From kindergarten through elementary, you might say I was a bit of a nerd. Miss Kane, my first grade teacher, always had nice things to say about me. *Pleasure to have in class,* was often one of the remarks on my report card. As long as my grades were good, my parents had no beef with me.

I learned from a young age that being a good student meant praise, accolades, and validation. Imagine Cookie Monster gobbling up applause, cheers, and compliments instead of cookies. That was me, and it tasted good as hell.

I was pretty ambitious and always knew I wanted to go to college so that I could have the best chance at establishing a good career. Growing up in a half-Caribbean household with a Jamaican mom and a dad who grew up in the projects of Harlem, NY, education always came first. Mom made sure homework was done, and Dad made sure my bookshelf was always full.

"Work hard" and "Get your education; they can never take that from you" were the two comments I heard most growing up. My wise Jamaican grandmother would say, "If yuh want good, yuh nose haffa run." The late Barbara Davis wanted a good life for her children and her children's children. She knew that in order to achieve your dreams, you had to put in the work and persevere until you reached your goals. Whether you liked the work or not didn't really matter as long as you could earn a living.

One of the first jobs my grandmother took when she emigrated to the US was as a domestic worker taking care of a family of four. She did this for several years, even while her own children were still in Jamaica, until she could send for them. Much later, she changed jobs and worked the overnight shift as a janitorial custodian at a big health insurance firm. It wasn't much money, the hours were long, and the work was backbreaking, but it was a job where she could make an honest living and support her family. She worked hard her entire life, right up until she got sick and couldn't work anymore. As a Black Caribbean woman with no formal education she was already limited with options, but she was brilliant at making the most of what she had.

Looking back decades later, I can see the opportunities and the options I was able to have because of the women who came before me. They endured so much so that I wouldn't have to. But because the stacks have always been against people of color, they could not protect me from walking into workspaces that were not designed for Black women to thrive. Arriving onto the corporate scene as a professional, degreed Black woman in my twenties where I thought opportunities would be available to me, was nothing but a rude awakening. No matter how smart, ambitious, and dedicated we are, it's hard for Black women in the workplace to thrive when we don't see ourselves as part of the company culture. It's hard to find joy and fulfillment in your work if you have to bend and contort yourself to be treated equitably or have to prove time and time again that you *do* deserve a seat at the table. We follow a rule book written by old rich, white men in order to achieve the American dream, and not surprisingly we are met with roadblock after roadblock.

Consider the facts: Black women make up a small minority in most corporate workspaces, and are typically not represented in senior leadership roles, are less likely to be promoted, or even groomed for promotion. According to "The State of Black Women in Corporate," a study conducted by *Lean In* in 2020:

> For every 100 men promoted to manager, only 58 Black women are promoted, despite the fact that Black women ask for promotions at the same rate as men. And for every 100 men hired into manager roles, only 64 Black women are hired.[2]

This is why I believe so many of us end up leaving corporate spaces to start a business and create something of our own. Why stay in a company where our talents are underutilized and underappreciated when we can

---

2 "The State of Black Women in Corporate America," report, *Lean In*, 2020, accessed January 16, 2023, https://leanin.org/research/state-of-black-women-in-corporate-america/introduction.

create our own damn company? I grew tired of working tirelessly for companies when it was clear they did not value me or have an interest in my advancement. It was one of the reasons I left and dedicated the last decade of my work toward helping women—particularly Black women—reevaluate their career choices. I aim to help us see our careers not as something we do just to survive, but as a pathway toward greater freedom and fulfillment.

Many of us go an entire lifetime without pausing to ask what *we* want. We live in a busy society and are constantly on the go from one thing to the next. "Busyness" reigns supreme. We get trapped in the cycle of "checking the career box" without questioning if the box was even ours to begin with. It's maddening to live your entire life that way. For many of us, the boxes generally look like this:

- ❑ Go to school.
- ❑ Get a good job.
- ❑ Make a lot of money.
- ❑ Find a nice partner. Double points if they've got a good job. Do all of this, preferably, before you're thirty.
- ❑ Fall in love.
- ❑ Get married. Start a family.
- ❑ Climb the corporate ladder.
- ❑ Buy a house in the burbs.
- ❑ Retire with a good pension.
- ❑ After you've checked all these items off your list, then go live your life and do what you really want.

Sound familiar?

Now, don't get me wrong. These are worthy boxes to check off. They represent comfort, stability, hard work, and milestones that indicate progress and happiness. It's the American Dream! Surely, if you are working towards these things and checking your boxes, it must mean that you are "successful" and winning at life. The problem with this formula is the assumption that the road to success is available to everybody equally and that this dream is what everyone wants. And most importantly, it doesn't take into account that sometimes things change; you can at any point change your mind and decide that some of these things are no longer important to you.

Every couple of years, the Gallup Poll reminds us that the majority of employees are actively disengaged or unhappy in their jobs. Year after year, in my consulting practice, I see companies struggle with retention as they continue to lose out on their best talent, who either move on to new jobs or leave the corporate grind all together. Career dissatisfaction is a universal experience that many of us can relate to. But it pains me to know that the Black women included in that seventy percent are most likely unhappy due in part to workplace trauma. Particularly when we hit what should be the prime of our careers, we slide into plateaus instead, becoming jaded by corporate life. We spend years doing what we think we need to do to get ahead, only to find ourselves stuck.

At some point in your career, you'll get stuck. It happens and it's quite normal. I call it a *career crossroads*. It's when you've been in the same career trajectory for years until you hit a fork in the road, or something causes you to reevaluate and change directions. The fork can take many forms, like suddenly being laid off, having to be a caretaker for your aging parents, becoming a parent, or simply outgrowing your role and desiring more out of a career. Most times, you'll have to decide whether you're going to stay to your left or veer right. The left represents all you know; it's the familiar, more predictable path. To the right is the unknown: the path representing change and uncertainty. You sense that you should go right and make a change because it could possibly lead you to everything you've ever wanted and dreamed of. Only thing is, it's scary as hell.

While you're standing at this proverbial crossroad, you feel uneasy. A quiet stirring inside signals something may need to change. You feel

the stirring late at night before bed, especially on Sunday evenings before
the work week starts and most definitely in the morning as you dread
returning to the office. Hello, Sunday scaries! Running yourself into
the ground at work every day for years is finally starting to wear thin.
You barely notice how you've been burning the candle at both ends and
pushing your body beyond the brink. You don't have time for much else
in your life, but the sad part is that you don't recognize it because it's just
become a normal part of working. You don't really see the struggle that
you're in. But your body does. Consider that the constant high blood
pressure might be tied to the stress of your toxic job.

As Black women, staying in a draining job takes a toll on our mental
health, causing stress levels to rise, and keeping us in a constant state of
anxiety. You can start to question whether you are doing enough at work,
and in response, you work harder and longer and increase deprivation.
Joy and purpose fade from work. Creativity takes a hit; fun and joy is
only reserved for the weekend. The longer the situation remains, the
greater burnout grows until exhaustion becomes the new normal.

It's only a matter of time until you reach the career crossroads and
realize that you can either play it safe and keep doing what you've always
done, or you can take a leap of faith and center your dreams again.

Dreaming Ourselves Free

Many of us have lost our ability to dream. When we think of the
word *dream,* it evokes a sense of imagination, fantasy, playfulness, and
illusion. It can also feel childlike, illogical, unrealistic, unattainable, or
too good to be true. Do you remember the game Candy Land? It was
my favorite game to play as a kid. I still remember the boardgame was
painted with fluffy clouds, candy canes, lollipops, butterflies, and these
happy-ass white kids. Playing felt like being in a dream to my five-year-
old self. All my favorite candies to eat and houses made of ice cream all
together in one place, even if it wasn't real. This is what we think when
we hear the word dream—a fairy tale. To take it further, our favorite
Biggie lyric tells us about his career, "It was all a dream" he went, "from

negative to positive" Who we become all starts with a dream.

Perhaps clichés like, "Follow your dreams," and, "Dream big," have become hollow. We've instead chosen time and again to be "realistic" and follow the familiar path. Over time, relying too much on being realistic takes the place of creativity and out-of-the-box thinking. How do we follow our dreams when there are bills to pay, and our "real" jobs have taken six figures of school tuition to achieve? The struggle is real.

When I reached my mid-to-late thirties, I often thought about the women in my family whom I grew up around. Many of them became mothers in their early twenties. My mother had my brother at twenty years old, and five years later, she had me. The only dream she had at the time was keeping us kids fed. That was about the only dream she could "allow" herself to have because once you have kids, mama's dreams go on hold. It was the cards she was dealt. I could not imagine having children at the age my mom had us; still so many young women become mothers and caregivers, sometimes not by choice. Now that I'm older, I can appreciate how much my mother sacrificed for us. It actually motivates me now as an adult to never take for granted the privileges and opportunities I have because many aren't afforded those same choices available to me.

You may have seen on t-shirts or spray painted in Black communities the saying, "I am my ancestors' wildest dreams." I reflect on those words often, visualizing my foremothers who broke barriers just for me to be here. My ancestors who were denied their dreams for four hundred years. Your ancestors created a path of opportunity for you, so you can choose your dreams in honor of them.

I want to acknowledge the privilege that comes with being able to go after your dreams. Not everyone is in a position to quit their jobs to follow their dreams, especially if they have aging parents to take care of and need that steady paycheck, or if they experience chronic health challenges that need support from an employer's health insurance plan. What we imagine and the dreams we yearn for will look different for everyone depending upon their situation. While following dreams may not look the same for everyone, we all can carve a little space for our desires to exist, be heard and be brought to light. Those of us who are in positions of privilege must do all we can to pave the way for others. None of us are free until we all are.

A Rude Awakening

I started my first real job out of college in 2003. I had graduated with honors from an HBCU with a degree in business management,[3] and I was finally ready to enter the world as a real, live working woman. I was offered an amazing opportunity working on a team responsible for enhancing the surgical unit through the collection of patient data. We used hundreds of data points to determine how to improve the overall quality of patient care. Pretty cool, right? I thought so too. I was thrilled to have a job and be in the working professional world.

I was the only person of color in my office except for an Asian woman whom I'll call "Liane." Liane quit not long after I started. I never knew the reason she decided to leave, but I witnessed a lot of tension and animosity towards her by my coworkers, especially one who happened to be a white, conservative woman. This woman viewed Liane as inept even though they shared the same credentials and years of experience. Liane was often treated poorly by others at work. She was deliberately left out when it came to office communications and social events. At the time, I never understood why people were so hostile to her. To me, she did her job just as well as anyone else, but colleagues seemed to want to punish her.

As a new employee and the only Black woman, I didn't want to be treated like Liane. I wanted to be welcomed and accepted, so I did everything I could to put my best foot forward. I was eager to prove myself. I was constantly asking questions so I could learn the job and raised my hand to take on new assignments.

---

3   HBCU stands for Historically Black College or University. Established prior to the 1964 Civil Rights Act, these institutions were aimed at providing educational opportunities for the advancement of African Americans.

I even wanted to dress the part. One of the things that makes me feel most confident is dressing well and looking put together. In the first few weeks of being on the job I observed the office attire which I quickly learned was mostly business casual. But I didn't want to just blend in, I wanted to stand out. I mean, I already stood out as one of the only women of color, but I wanted to step it up and dress more like the Directors and those I saw in senior level positions. They say dress for the job you want, and I took that to heart. I spent a lot of time at shopping malls to buy the right business attire. I was so determined to look the part at my first professional job. I wanted to be taken seriously and prove to management that they had hired the right person.

Despite being, in my opinion, one of the best dressed people in the office, even fresh pantsuits didn't make me feel any less invisible. While I wasn't mistreated outright like Liane was, I felt largely unseen by my coworkers and especially my managers. At times I felt like the office pet. I was well-liked by colleagues but never really taken seriously or respected for my contributions. It was as if I was the "shiny new thing" in the office that people liked having around but needed to keep at bay. While I was in an entry level role, I constantly communicated my desire for bigger assignments to my manager. I even shared my goals with coworkers, thinking they were more tenured and could vouch for me. But I was constantly saddled with administrative, tedious work. They had no interest in my advancement unless it benefited them. Being the nice, quiet Black woman in the office, I didn't want to rock the boat, so I just rolled with it.

On paper, having a degree and getting a good job with great benefits and a steady paycheck meant I was well on my way in the box-checking department. A sprightly millennial in her early twenties couldn't get more successful than that! Despite how I felt at work, if you had asked me back then what success meant to me, I would have thought that was it. But deep down, I was on a hamster wheel and increasingly losing touch with who I was and what I wanted to be. Back then, my work identity, title, my degree, and my accomplishments—they were everything that mattered. I wanted people to see that I made it. Being a first generation woman in the corporate world came with a lot of pressure but was only the tip of the iceberg. I would soon learn just how treacherous the waters would get.

Being one of very few Black women in the office started to wear on me. Back then, diversity was not the workplace buzzword that it is today. Every day I went to work feeling like I had to armor up. I did that with the way I wore my hair (always chemically straightened) and how I dressed—constantly being mistaken for the *other* Black girl—and I even changed the radio station from hip hop and R&B to something I thought my coworkers would like whenever they rode any where with me. Every day, in order to get by, I had to minimize the parts of me that made me who I was. I wanted to see more people who looked like me in the business world and in the office. I craved it.

After about two years of being underutilized at my job at the hospital, I decided to go back to school for my MBA. Many of my colleagues already had masters degrees, so I thought, clearly that's the reason I'm not being considered for advancement because I didn't have an advanced degree. Duh! It didn't matter that I was putting myself in more tuition debt; remember, dog with a bone. I was willing to do whatever it took to make it.

Attending business school in Long Island, an already predominantly white county, was my first, small taste of real diversity in a post college, professional setting. The classrooms were majority white but had more people of color than I was used to seeing at work, not to mention international students. It felt like mecca: a world I wanted to be in, full of diverse faces, ethnicities, cultural backgrounds, and world experiences.

Right around the time I graduated from business school, I started thinking about my next career move. I packed up my things and moved to New York City; the epicenter of all commerce.

I'm not going to lie. Moving to the big city from the quiet suburbs was a flex. I felt like a rock star renegade who was young, ambitious, and living in the concrete jungle where dreams are made—this time with a shiny MBA degree. What?! Couldn't tell me nothing! Alicia Keys and Jay-Z would be proud. If I wasn't being valued at my last job, there were plenty of other companies in the big city that would appreciate me, I thought.

I quickly landed another job, this time as an analyst within the tech department at a posh marketing firm. The company took up an entire floor in a tall, brown building in Midtown East. I still remember damn near breaking my neck as I looked up from the street at how tall my new office building was. It seemed to touch the clouds; it was taller than any building I'd seen at that point. I was making about ten thousand dollars more in my salary, clearly I was raking in the dough so I immediately got a large one-bedroom apartment in Queens that was about a thirty-minute subway commute to the office. I hit the ground running at my new job. On weeknights, I laughed it up with my coworkers during happy hours, and on weekends, I hung out in Manhattan's trendiest bars and clubs. I was doing alright, and life felt really good.

Although switching from my job in Long Island to a new gig in the city barely yielded the multicultural hub I was seeking in the workplace, outside of the office was where I got to meet interesting new people from all over the world. I was exposed to new cultures and had fascinating conversations with people from all walks of life who expanded my world view—all within a bustling city. I was totally in love with my life.

But my career? That was another story.

Inside the walls of that tall, brown high-rise building, I was surviving, not thriving. Monday through Friday, I worked ten, sometimes twelve hours behind a desk and in client meetings. That doesn't include the work I took home with me. On the one hand, while the people I worked with were OK, I couldn't help but feel the pressure to fit in and never be a threat. Dress the part, look the part, never question authority, and always speak in your "professional voice" (you know the voice I'm talking about ladies). Somehow I knew that these were the silent rules to be accepted into their club. Their club consisted of mostly cis, white, hetero, men with button downs and khaki pants. But that's tech for ya!

These men were clearly following the same rule book—one written for them and by them to ensure their rise to corporate power. My team was all men, with the exception of one other woman and myself. She seemed to play in the boys' club pretty well. But I watched this woman who was smart and extremely qualified be passed over for promotion each year. I quickly caught on to what was happening, but I just grew accustomed to the way things were.

There is a certain type of business persona that is praised and valued more than any other type. This persona is often dominating and asserts itself forcefully in leadership. It rules with an iron fist, is cold and calculating, and is determined to win at any cost. This persona is not compassionate and certainly doesn't listen or take others into consideration unless they think the others are like them. Back then, this iron-fisted persona is one I thought I had to wear in order to be successful. So, I played along or at least tried to; I never showed vulnerability and stuffed down my creative, playful side (read: the unwelcomed parts of myself). I was seeking validation from others, yet devaluing myself in the process. I was shrinking and minimizing so that I wouldn't scare others off or dare make anyone uncomfortable.

I had always struggled with people pleasing, but the people I strove to please always seemed to be white men and women, particularly those in powerful positions. I believed that staying on their good side and prioritizing their comfort made the difference between having a job or not. That meant being agreeable, going above and beyond, even when it wasn't noticed, not being allowed to make a mistake, and saying the right thing in the right way. Being one of the only Black women at the company kept me in continual survival mode. That's a hard game to play 365 days year after year, and after a while, it wears on your soul and mental health.

Working for a toxic boss created one of the most defining experiences in my career. Too often, I was talked down to, yelled at, and made to feel inferior. Whenever he turned the corner in the mornings to come into the office, I was instantly stricken by his presence. My boss was known for being tough, but none of my coworkers had gone through anything remotely similar to the mistreatment I received. I was incredibly miserable every day, and I usually left work in tears. At the time, my younger self didn't see the situation as toxic. I just thought that was how corporate life worked in fast-paced New York City, and that I should just suck it up. If I continued to work hard like my grandmother taught me, things would eventually get better. I chalked up my experience to the misfortune of having a bad boss.

But looking back, there certainly was something more going on.

When you are the only person of color, you become super-aware that you are different and how that difference causes the people around you to be uncomfortable. I wanted to believe the color of my skin was never a factor in how I was treated because, hey, racism is over, right? But looking back, it's as clear as day: my bad boss did not want me to forget his power and influence over me.

He was effective. I recall one particular instance when he harshly criticized my work in front of everyone. I honestly don't remember his exact words, but I remember how I felt—completely tense and unable to find my words to respond to his anger-induced interrogation. "What the hell do I pay you for?" he barked at me. I just sat across from his desk in silence as he reamed me out. It would be another year of enduring a pit in my stomach every Sunday night and dwindling self-esteem before I eventually left to find a new job.

I moved on to a new job with a fancier title and a small bump in salary. I didn't care about the pay, I just needed to get myself out of there. Admittedly though, after working with a toxic boss for two years, my confidence had taken a hit. I thought something was wrong with me, that I had done a bad job, and that I would find some way to screw up in my new role. I had really internalized the mistreatment and snide comments about my performance from my former boss and brought it into this new job.

Different job, same bullsh*t. On the outside, everything looked great. I had more responsibility. I got along well with my coworkers, managed several large client accounts, accepted every opportunity to grow professionally, and developed my leadership skills. But again, keeping up with the demands of the job, with little support, and constantly trying to prove that I was capable taxed my emotional reserves. I was drowning but couldn't let it show. Showing up for work became a struggle, and my anxiety was constantly on high.

I commuted to work on a packed rush hour train every morning and returned exhausted every night, only to do it all over again the next day. It went on like this for years. I dreaded going to work and conforming to the role I thought I had to take to eventually one day being able to say it was all worth it. By the time I got to my near-thirties, I felt completely out of touch with my true self. *How did I get here? Where am I going? Is this what I really want?* These were the questions I struggled with. I had reached my *career crossroad.*

But one day, something changed during my normal commute to work on a packed train, heading into the office just as I had done the day before and the day before that. On this particular day, I felt numb. Essentially, I was in autopilot mode, and honestly, I had been coasting there for awhile. Around that time, I turned to self-help books and blogs to find out more about the unhappiness I felt. These resources helped me see that being in J-O-B mode for the past several years had depleted me of something I never once stopped to consider: my sense of purpose. Despite checking all the boxes, I still felt like I was missing something. I became curious about what my purpose was. I deeply craved it, but I wasn't quite sure what it meant or what that would even look like in my life. The people on the cover of these self-help books seemed to be happy, so they must've had purpose in their lives. So, what was mine?

Purpose

Let's pause and check in. What's coming up for you when you read the word *purpose*? The idea of having a purpose can sometimes seem lofty and intimidating. Some people shy away from that word, some avoid it all together, and some haven't really slowed down enough to consider what truly living with purpose could mean. Wherever you find yourself is okay. I'd like to share my perspective on it. Keep what resonates with you and leave the rest.

I believe living with purpose means walking through life with intention and an awareness of who and what you are. It means knowing what you believe in and how your perspectives serve the greater good. Living with purpose means making choices that align with your truth regardless of the situation you find yourself in. It means being present with the constant unfolding of life as it changes and takes on new shapes. Our purpose consists of moments that, when strung together, reveal the *who*, the *what*, and the *why* of our lives.

Living with purpose isn't always a warm and fuzzy cloud-parting experience; sometimes it's tumultuous. It's easy to think living with purpose means having a great new job or business, a successful romantic relationship, and more money in the bank. But what if your purpose at this moment is to be in the soul-sucking job? To be unemployed? To be in the toxic relationship? To have a negative bank balance? To be reading these words right now?

I have experienced every last one of these situations before, and at the time, it seemed like I would never get through them. But they were only temporary, circumstances I had to go through in order to learn what I needed to learn from them. I believe that sometimes moments of personal turmoil are designed to stretch you, prepare you, and guide you into the next chapter of your journey, and thus, deeper into your sense of purpose. This is not to say we need to endure struggle in order to have nice things, but I do believe hard times can sometimes serve a purpose.

Purpose is often a paradox. It includes the things we run *from* and things we run *toward*. It is the light and the darkness of the human experience. For most of us, the word *purpose* can be intimidating. If someone asks the question, "What is your purpose?" and your response is, "I don't know," that can feel scary. Even if we believe we know the answer to that question, doubt lingers. It may sound like "What if I'm wrong?" or "I'm not good enough."

To that I say, there is power in learning to live in the unknown. We don't always need to chase down a specific answer to "figure out" what our purpose is. Perhaps in uncertain moments, our purpose is to accept the mystery with a sense of curiosity. Answers can come to you on the yoga mat, while reading a book, in mid-conversation, or if you're like me, while peering out of your office window.

One morning in the summer of 2010, I walked into my office building and pressed thirty-three, the elevator button for my floor. As I rode up to my office, I could feel my shallow breath. My mind, for once, was completely quiet. No racing thoughts about the workday ahead, just clear and serene silence. The elevator doors opened to reveal the company logo displayed against the glass doors in front of me. I walked out of the elevator and down the hall into my office without saying a word to anyone and closed the door behind me.

I set my bag down on the chair next to my desk and walked over to the window. I peered out at the bright, sunny sky and then down at the sidewalk. The scene below revealed a normal Monday morning with cars and trucks backed up in traffic, blaring horns, and delivery men making their rounds. I looked up and down the avenue filled with crowds of people hurriedly going to work. As I continued to look through the window, taking in the scene that I was a part of just a moment ago, it dawned on me: this is *not* what I want. My box checking hadn't quite panned out the way I thought.

WTF?

That fateful day in front of the window was my wake-up call. It was as though, in that moment, life opened my eyes. For the first time, I could see things for what they really were.

Many times, we want to hit the snooze button when we realize something in our lives must change. Or we downright ignore the urge. But when we don't pay attention to those gentle wake-up calls, life will take matters into its own hands, and—out of love—offer a violent shove.

I wish I could tell you that after that wake-up call, it all became clear, I quit my job and rode off into the sunset. But it didn't quite happen that way. I had bills to pay, and I'd grown accustomed to receiving a paycheck every two weeks. I was afraid to leave that behind. I continued to stay at my job and tried to ignore the deep feelings of unease and discontent, hoping they would disappear. But I underestimated the situation; when you know something, you can't un-know it. And trying to push through or ignore it completely will not make the problem go away. Eventually, you will have to deal with it.

I stayed unhappy in my job for a long time, but this time I knew the answer wasn't to just find another job. I was afraid another job would bring more of the same, so I stayed put. But life gave me a big ol' shove that year.

Several months after my WTF moment, I was fired. Just like that, the rug was pulled out from under me. My cushy job, my paycheck on the first and the fifteenth, my health insurance, the 401k, and all of my other security blankets were gone. It seemed so sudden and out of the blue, but in reality, I was burnt out and wasn't performing my best. I was quiet quitting before quiet quitting was a thing. How could I show up at a company that clearly did not want to show up for me? How could I thrive in a space that preferred I minimize and shrink myself than acknowledge that I exist?

In hindsight, it took being fired to see that I had accumulated a lot of trauma throughout my years in the corporate world, and my heart wasn't in it any more. I needed that big ol' shove to shake me up so that I could heal and discover who I really was, what I wanted, and what was possible.

Too many of us spend time doing work we don't believe in. We spend too many waking hours working until eventually, our soul switches off and our brain goes into autopilot. Months and years go by like this until something smacks us and grabs our attention. It isn't until the world turns upside down that we begin to re-evaluate what is important in our lives and what we truly want.

But why do we wait until shit hits the fan, the economy crashes, we get laid off, we lose a loved one, have our own health scare, or face a pandemic to start thinking about what truly matters?

Why?

Because pain is the ultimate motivator.

The Shake-Up

Fast forward to the 2016 election stirred a wave of emotions ranging from shock and outrage to *what the fuck do we do now?* It's as if the proverbial rug for a life of complacency was pulled out from under us A call to action ensued for many of us. We got involved, became aware, and mobilized around issues that impacted us all.

We are seeing it on a grander collective scale within social movements when it comes to women's rights, the rise of Black feminist ideologies, and the intersection of gender, race, and sexual orientation. From Black Lives Matter, to Time's Up, to Me Too, movements are calling us back to our humanity and continuing the work of dismantling a system that no longer works for us.

My favorite quote by Anais Nin says, "And the day came when the risk to remain tight in a bud was more painful than the risk it took to blossom."

When it would be easier to continue going down a comfortable, familiar path, to remain tight in that bud, we must ask ourselves: at what cost? Purposefully choosing how we want to live, work, and build in a world that wants us to simply follow the status quo is a radical act.

Pushing back on the status quo—or leaving the comfort zone—has long been frowned upon and, especially for Black folks, could literally cost our lives. It's called the comfort zone for a reason. For Black women, we were taught as a survival skill not to rock the boat. There is much more at stake for us. So we have developed high tolerances for staying in uncomfortable situations; whether it's a toxic job or toxic relationship, I have seen us remain seated even when everything around us is in flames. We are a resilient bunch but almost to a fault. Nothing about denying your dreams or putting up with less than you deserve is normal. When it comes to comfort zones, nothing ever grows there.

When I was fired, I finally realized I had been given the freedom to dream bigger and explore what I truly wanted. I wanted to explore my creativity. I wanted to get to know myself on a deeper level and listen to my heart without the distractions of a traumatic workplace. I needed to heal my soul. I wanted to change the world and make our work culture a little less destructive. I was frustrated that so many of us get so little value from our jobs and suffer the toll they take on our mental health. Unrealistic expectations, the grind, and the pressure to produce at any cost are built into work culture. It adversely impacts minority groups the hardest.

We spend more waking hours in our jobs than anywhere else—on average, 90,000 hours over a lifetime. A third of our lives, in fact, are spent at work. Even more if you include hours of unpaid housework and caregiving after the traditional workday ends. For a lot of us, especially people of color, that means spending a third of our lives or more in survival mode, drained and burnt out. I don't know about you, but I'm pretty sure that's not what was meant for our lives.

On the morning human resources (HR) brought me into the office, I sat in stunned silence as I heard the announcement: "We're letting you go, Ariane. You are terminated effective today. Please proceed to the lobby and someone will bring your belongings down to you."

I sat across from the HR manager under fluorescent lights, tightness in my belly forming, feeling incredibly embarrassed. I was not permitted to return to my desk to collect my own things; someone would bring them out to me outside of the building. It was as though they were doing me a favor by getting my stuff, so I would not have to face my coworkers after being let go. But it felt more like I was being treated like a criminal. Like everyone at the office except me had known I was being fired.

I waited at the front door of the lobby until they brought the personal items from my desk, including my own pocketbook. I walked to the parking lot, got in my car, and sat there, still not fully registering what had just happened. I drove home in silence, completely zoned out, staring only at the road ahead of me. So many things swirled through my mind at once. I had never been let go from a job before. What was happening to me? What was I going to do? What would people think? Would I be disappointing my mother? My family? How would I explain this?

I was in a daze, angry but also relieved. Deep down I knew that being let go might have been the blessing in disguise that I was secretly hoping for: to be free from the nine-to-five hustle and away from the place that caused me so much stress.

I thought long and hard about my situation. I had a great résumé. I was employable and could probably get another job easily. But I wanted to chart a new course and do something different. I gave myself permission to take it slow and figure out my next steps, but deep down I already knew.

When I finally arrived home early that afternoon, I headed for my laptop. *Maybe it's time for me to start my own business.* I definitely didn't have all my ducks in a row, but I had to take the leap. While I made a lot of mistakes and fell on my butt more times than I care to count, I learned so much about building a dream from scratch and daring to do what most would call crazy.

At the time, all I knew was that I needed to walk away from a toxic situation. If this business thing didn't work out, there was always Plan B—I could always get another J-O-B. In my heart, I knew I never wanted to go back to that, so I HAD to make it work.

The New Truth about Dreams

It's time to stop thinking about our dreams as flights of fantasy; *they are a call to action.* Our dreams represent an invitation, a starting point for creating change, awakening to something new, and realizing a new reality that does not yet exist. Our dreams can take many forms: a project, an idea, or a solution to a problem. Regardless, they are an impetus for change.

Frequently, our dreams require something of us that we often don't believe we possess. We tend to brush off our dreams or believe they are impossible because we don't yet have the tools or the know-how to begin.

But that is what's so special about dreaming. Dreams call us to become a new version of ourselves, and through this, we learn who we really are.

Dreams don't always come true, at least not in the way we expect them to. However, maybe dreams aren't so much about acquiring or achieving what we want but about becoming the person we know we can be. Maybe deep down we know what we are truly capable of, even though we convince ourselves otherwise. The whole point of dreaming is to fantasize and imagine making what seems impossible, *possible*. Our dreams represent the unrestricted and limitless versions of ourselves and what we're capable of.

Because we fear failure, we tend to put limits around our dreams. We dream—but not too big—injecting some form of "realistic" thinking to make sure our dreams can be contained and measured. We dream safely so that if we fail, we won't be too disappointed or can prove to ourselves why going after the silly thing was a bad idea anyway.

But if your dreams don't scare you, you're not dreaming big enough.

When a Black woman decides to go for her dreams and play a bigger game in her own life, it's like a ripple effect for other Black women in her circle to do the same. I've been encouraged by so many women throughout my career, many of whom had no idea I looked up to them. Similarly, when I decided to become an entrepreneur, I heard from other women who decided to start their own businesses after seeing what I had done.

A former colleague, someone I had worked with years before I started my company, emailed me to let me know that she had been following my journey. She had finally decided to leave her full-time job to start her own branding firm! She was not happy in her employment situation and decided she could make more money with her own clients. I couldn't have been more thrilled for her, and I felt honored to know that I played even a small part in her decision to break free.

In my own family, older relatives would suddenly confide in me about hidden passions and dreams that they had never spoken of before. I felt honored to hold their stories. They helped me realize the powerful impact we have on each other. It's magic! Someone will always be watching what we do and the choices we make, so we are inspiring others in their lives whether we realize it or not.

As more and more Black women break down barriers and show what is possible, we give others permission to do the same. Like the first person to go out onto the dance floor and start dancing (totally me when the dj plays the electric slide), one person joins, then another, and eventually the dance floor is full of party people dancing the night away. It only takes one person to ignite change in others.

Every woman intuitively knows what that next step is for her. It is a very personal journey. It might mean starting a new business, leaving the dead-end job, doing a TED Talk, taking the job across the country because she feels in her heart that it's the right move, speaking her mind openly in the boardroom, sharing new ideas with the power to change the course of traditionally held views, or just getting out of her head and trusting herself.

The impact we have on one another is far greater than we could ever imagine. Being in a community of like-minded, trailblazing women who are going for it sparks something within us. The fire in our bellies roars to a flame, and we are inspired to get out there, be our best selves, and do our best work.

The road toward living our dreams is imperfect, paved with setbacks, longer than expected wait times, and dark nights of the soul. Still, we march on. It takes courage to do this kind of work, to follow a dream, to make an impact, to let go of comfort, risk failure and disappointment, and believe in an idea so fiercely that we would die for it.

You have to do the thing that calls to your soul. It's no longer an option to deny your dreams. You cannot remain in an unfulfilling job, make excuses, listen to your fears, and yield to circumstances that keep you blocked every day. You must become loyal to your dreams instead of your fears. Part of going for your dreams means becoming curious about who you are and the work you want to do in this world—even if your dreams and passions aren't terribly clear. There is no greater time to start exploring them than right now.

So where *do* we start? How do we begin to shift out of our old ways of thinking about careers and doing work that matters? How do we begin to align with a greater sense of purpose and dare to dream more fully?

We must first acknowledge and accept when we have drifted away from our deepest values and visions through choices that are not our own. We need to ask where we have been checking boxes instead of living and determine what a life of purpose truly looks like. Ask yourself: What am I tolerating right now? What am I ready to walk away from in order to create the life I truly want?

The answers to these questions come with time and patience. They certainly don't come overnight, but when you're willing to explore them through the lens of curiosity, without judgment or a rush to *hurry up and figure it out*, you ease into what's possible.

Through deep inquiry and self-reflection, you can learn to tune out external distractions and begin listening to your internal voice. It's the best way to begin to see purpose more clearly. Only then will you be able to define success on your own terms rather than something based on status, prestige, and what's on your résumé.

Listening to your inner voice allows you to truly see the stories you bought into and evaluate whether they continue to serve you. Doing the work of dismantling antiquated thinking modes allows you to clear away what no longer works and move into what is really true for you as an individual. It's called doing your *right work*.

Will this path be easy? Absolutely not. Change never is. You will likely encounter a lot of resistance, either your own or from those around you. Dreaming on purpose is not for the faint of heart, but it is absolutely one of the most rewarding journeys you could ever take.

Purpose to Practice

When it comes to making a change in your career, whether it's changing jobs, getting a promotion or starting a new business on the side, start by reevaluating your priorities. Identify what's important to you now. Grab your journal, and let's start with a *then and now* exercise.

1. **What were your top career priorities five to ten years ago?** How did they inform your decisions back then about career choices and the jobs you've had? Examples can be: Making money, security/ having a steady paycheck, pleasing your family, or taking a job just to have one.

2. **Write down your current top five priorities for your life and career today.** Examples might include more freedom in your schedule, time to do more creative work, or earning more money.

3. **Take some time to define your current values.** Referring to the list below, identify your top three, and define what they mean to you. Use the example that follows as a guide.

Humor	Fairness	Friendship
Love	Happiness	Security
Achievement	Balance	Privacy
Faith	Gratitude	Service to others
Excellence	Freedom	Adventure
Kindness	Family	Power
Loyalty	Harmony	Courage
Responsibility	Rest	Authenticity
Humility	Integrity	Independence
Health	Impact	Commitment
Creativity	Knowledge	Passion
Resilience	Money	Drive

Value	Definition	One action I will do this week to align with this value is . . .
Example: Peace	To no longer worry about things I cannot control	I will reserve ten minutes of quiet time during my work day just for myself.

Chapter 2
TAKING THE LEAP

WHILE SOME COLLEGE KIDS WENT on spring break, I spent time at home sitting on my front stoop with a thick *International Business* textbook in my lap, daydreaming of possibilities. I always loved the study of business and envisioned myself working at a big company one day. I saw myself as a high-powered businesswoman, wearing heels and pantsuits, walking through hallways, commanding respect, and pointing to graphs and charts while talking to audiences about revenues and growth projections. I studied business in college and grad school, but being the CEO of my *own* business, never once crossed my mind.

I started a business at the age of twenty-nine. This was back when entrepreneurship wasn't the sexy job title it is today. I knew zero people doing what I did. There were no YouTube tutorials showing me how to be an entrepreneur, no e-courses, no TikTok's; social media wasn't the wellspring of information that it is today. Even a degree in business and years of corporate experience did not prepare me for what it would be like as a budding entrepreneur in the real world, particularly in New York City. Back then, leaving your cushy corporate job to start a risky business venture was considered career suicide. Yet there I was.

In some ways I was lucky. I was young and single, had no children, and had a higher tolerance for risk. I could take risks in ways that others with a family, children, and other obligations could not. For that, I am extremely grateful. I have so much respect for those who started businesses while holding it down as a wife and mother—perhaps even as a means of survival. Seriously, how do you do it?

About two years before I was let go from my last corporate job, I started freelancing as a photographer. What began as a hobby to counter stress from my full-time job gradually turned into a side hustle. On nights and weekends, I moonlighted, shooting weddings and headshots for paying clients. I loved being hired for work that I actually enjoyed doing, and I appreciated the freedom it gave me. It also gave me a break from the daily grind. It let me tap into another part of my brain in a creative way and gave me autonomy. I even took evening photography classes to improve my skills. I remember from time to time during some of my photo gigs thinking, *I could do this for a living.* But back then, I would not have considered myself an actual freelance photographer because I wasn't yet ready to take myself and my creative work seriously. I struggled with self-worth and valuing myself. Even though I was getting paid for my work, had a portfolio website and business cards, I didn't quite *own it* professionally. In my mind, it was just a side hustle and I still thought of myself as just a hobbyist photographer.

Freelancing taught me so much about what it was like to own a business, like how to get clients and make money. In time, my confidence as a photographer and business woman grew. When I was let go from my job, I was less afraid to start my own business full time because I had been doing it on the side for a while. Plus, thank God for a little naiveté; I didn't know what I didn't know. A little part of me was like, "How hard can it be?" I continued photographing weddings and headshots. I even did baby showers, birthday parties, corporate events, and bar mitzvahs. As a single woman living in one of the most expensive cities in the world, I took any job I could get to bring in money. The small savings from my corporate days wasn't going to last forever, so I had to hustle. Before I knew it, I was running a business! It was scrappy in the beginning, but I loved it, and it was mine.

Many times throughout the course of building my business, I was thrust into situations that called on a side of me I didn't know I had, one that managed problem-solving, negotiations, self-promotion, leading a team, product development, communicating powerfully, and selling myself time and time again. As someone who normally shies away from these types of things (self-promotion—yuck!), being forced to do it for my business taught me what I am truly capable of. In some ways, my business has been one of my greatest teachers.

Sometimes we limit our own thinking about what we can do based on the box we put ourselves in. As long as we keep ourselves in that box, we'll never know the true extent of our abilities. Entrepreneurship calls us to stretch into the unknown and activate dormant strengths. It makes us come alive.

I believe we attract the life experiences that we most need in order to learn and grow. Entrepreneurship challenges us to grow our capacity to learn, lead, and be transformed. Being a business owner brings experiences you just don't get when you're working for a company. If you are a creative person but aren't business savvy, you learn to build a logistical side of yourself that may not come naturally to you. Conversely, if you are detailed and number oriented, you'll learn to innovate and envision the bigger picture. In the beginning of my business career, I sucked at numbers. (My accountant loved me during tax time.) If I wanted my business to succeed, I had to learn how to truly think like a CEO and love all aspects of my business, not just the fun and sexy parts.

When We Take the Leap

Several years back, I took an informal Facebook poll asking women who had either started their own business or aspired to start one what their most compelling reason was for doing so. While many shared flexibility and work-life balance as the main reasons, a significant number also stated that their idea to become business owners was born out of a creative calling or a strong desire to solve a problem. They used words like *self-actualization* and *self-expression* and offered reasons along the lines of *making the world a better place, finding a sense of purpose,* and *living out their dreams.*

Taking the leap in any endeavor, whether it's in your career or a new relationship, can be adventurous and exciting. You're putting your heart on the line and trading in your comfort zone for something new and unpredictable. You will discover many things about yourself by taking the leap and by falling on your butt. Unfortunately, you cannot have one without the other. Leaving your comfort zone holds lessons that can only be learned if you're willing to fall, if you're willing to be uncomfortable, and if you're willing to be defined not by your failures but by whom you have become by conquering them. When you are the CEO of your own company, you always have to look ahead and create the vision of change you wish to see. You become responsible for creating a company that not only solves a problem but helps improve the lives of others. When you're in the business of helping people be a better version of themselves, the work becomes bigger than you. That's the beauty of being an entrepreneur.

Throughout the years, I've heard many stories from women about why they started their businesses. It's so much more than logos and sales. It's about handling those moments when life throws us curveballs, bettering ourselves and our communities, and impacting change for an entire industry.

After just a few months of starting her own business, one of my clients learned that her grandmother was in the hospital and needed major surgery. She was able to quickly hop on a plane and be by her grandmother's side, something that would have been more difficult to do had she still worked at her full-time office job. She told me how much being there meant to her, not only because she was close with her grandmother, but because it gave her the opportunity to take care of her grandmother in the ways her grandmother had taken care of her as a child.

Another client I worked with quit her job as a physician to go full time in her business. She started a consulting company after experiencing blatant racial inequities in the medical field that were causing harm to Black and brown communities.

A textile designer and first-time mom started her business simply to put herself and her daughter in a better financial position. After decades of creating designs for multimillion dollar companies and being underpaid for it, she realized her first commitment was to herself and to her family.

Now more than ever, women-owned businesses are on the rise. Nationwide, there are nearly 13 million women-owned businesses, and the number is increasing at inspiring rates year over year. For women of color, the stats are even more exciting. According to National Women's Business Council, women-owned businesses represented 42 percent of all US based firms in 2020.[4]

While the number of women-owned businesses are growing at an impressive rate, the number of firms owned by Black women grew by a stunning 164 percent since 2007. As of this writing, there are 2.6 million African American women-owned businesses in 2020, and most were owned by women aged thirty-five to fifty-four.[5]

As of February 2021, 275,000 women said "peace out" to their hard-earned careers, many of which were not by choice. The onset of COVID-19 left an indelible mark on the population's most essential part of the workforce. In December 2020, 154,000 Black women alone left the workforce. And according to the 2020 Women in the Workplace study,[6] one in four women are now considering leaving the workplace or downshifting their careers. When responsibilities like childcare, caring for aging parents, and maintaining the household all fall squarely on the shoulders of most working women, a health crisis or economic downturn always impacts women—especially Black women—the hardest.

---

4   Maddie Shepherd, "Women-owned businesses: Statistics and Overview," *Fundera*, updated December 16, 2020, https://www.fundera.com/resources/women-owned-business-statistics.

5   "State of African-American Owned Businesses," SCORE, February 25, 2020.

6   Ali Bohrer et al., "Women in the Workplace," report, LeanIn, McKinsey & Company, 2020, https://womenintheworkplace.com/2020.

So where does that leave one of the population's most vulnerable groups?

In a very powerful position to rebuild and drive economic prosperity through entrepreneurship.

When I started as a business owner, I was driven by the sense of freedom to create my own thing and play by my own rules. When I was working full time in corporate, I didn't feel that I could thrive as a cog in the wheel. There wasn't a clear path for me to advance, nor did I feel particularly valued for what I brought to the table. I wasn't making what I knew I could make as someone who was highly qualified with an advanced degree. I grew tired of always trying to "prove" myself.

Unfortunately, this type of scenario is common for most Black women who decide to leave the corporate space. Many women and racialized groups behind this trend of rapidly launching businesses started out of necessity. When faced with higher unemployment rates, long-term unemployment, and significant gender and racial pay gaps, women of color started businesses out of the need to survive more than anything else. They became business owners because they had to.

Entrepreneurship for Black women was a common path long before our generation. My great-grandmother had a small farm in Jamaica where she grew coffee and cocoa beans and sold them to the local grocery stores for a profit. She was the only woman in town doing this at the time, so in a sense, she saw an opportunity and cornered the market. My great-grandmother never worked for anyone else and, for years, was able to support herself and her children through the money she made from her business.

Madame C. J. Walker started her haircare business in the early 1900s out of personal necessity. She suffered from scalp irritations and made a product that was not on the market at the time. Madame C. J. Walker went on to become the first Black woman to run a million-dollar company in the US. What I love most about her story is how she bought supplies from other Black women entrepreneurs to help develop her product and gave money from her business to support Black movements of her time. She poured money back in our community; something our culture needs to do a better job at.

My beautiful friend and fellow business owner, a Latina woman who runs her own thriving digital design studio in Manhattan, shared that in the last two years, she has received her biggest client projects from those who deliberately sought her out as a minority-owned business. She competes in one of the most male-dominated industries around, and as a minority woman in tech, the odds are disproportionately stacked against her. However, as consumers become more mindful and intentional of whom we do business with, we can show support with our dollars. As a woman and woman of color in business, my friend has an advantage in the market and can now bring a level of visibility to her work like never before.

Many of my clients' stories concern women who had first worked traditional full-time jobs for many years, reaching senior positions in their companies before breaking out on their own. Some were forced out through internal politics; some experienced overt racism within the workplace and no longer felt safe. And some were inspired by their own children. One such woman started a touring and hospitality company when she noticed that her two middle-aged children weren't exposed to African culture within the classroom in the same way white students were exposed to European culture. As a mother who wanted her kids to know their family ancestry and heritage, she was inspired to build a company for people interested in learning more about Ghana and rediscovering their roots. She describes her company as not just a touring company, but travel for anyone who wants to experience an immersion of history and culture.

This woman is a mom, a wife, and now an entrepreneur. For her, the biggest transformation in becoming an entrepreneur is not just selling a service but putting herself out there, being seen, and becoming more visible as the voice of her company. In a sense, the world needs her to share her voice so that it can receive the beautiful gift her business offers. Clearly, minority women business owners are on the move. Self-made women have paved the way for all of us to shine.

The Changing Landscape

We are experiencing one of the most pivotal moments of our time, and it's an opportunity to actively create a better work world. The COVID-19 pandemic disrupted the world in a way we have never experienced before. It forced us to face a reality that existed well before the pandemic started; the old ways of working have led to burnout and unfulfillment. The only way forward now is to radically redefine the way we work. We are reevaluating and reconsidering what is important and identifying the changes we want to make in our lives and careers. Since 2020, studies have shown that at least one in three workers are considering leaving their jobs. Another sixty percent say they are rethinking their work. More than 4.4 million new businesses were created in the US, which has been the highest total on record according to the Census Bureau. These numbers were highest in Black communities where the pandemic hit the hardest.[7]

My prediction is that in less than ten years from now, the economy will have shifted, and independent workers will become the majority. Having a side hustle or side business will bring more job security than traditional full-time work. As we Black women are starting businesses, changing careers, (re)inventing ourselves, building communities, creating, innovating, and forging new paths, we are positioned at the forefront of the changing future of work. Although we still have a long way to go, we are positioned to close the pay and leadership gap. We are leading households and leveraging our buying and voting power. Our voices are being heard, and we are awakening to our dormant power. We are at the cusp of revolutionary change!

Now, with so many of us stepping into our power through entrepreneurship or senior leadership, we are in the best position to break

---

7   Lauren Dolan and Jason Carroll "Black Americans, hit hardest by the pandemic, feel they're hurt by both the virus and inequities tied to race," CNN, September 3, 2020, https://www.cnn.com/2020/09/03/us/race-disparities-coronavirus-six-months.

down barriers that represent an archaic, patriarchal system. We can create a working world that best reflects a more progressive, modern reality. And most importantly, we get to knock down the walls for the generations following us.

The pandemic showed us how fragile we really are as a society. Job security can be taken away at any second. With inflation and warnings of going into a recession, we will continue to see businesses cut costs in the form of layoffs. We now have the opportunity to look at ourselves and reexamine what we truly want and demand what is important to us. As technology advances and we become a more globalized society, we have a greater number of options for how we build our careers and leadership, both inside and outside of corporate walls.

Reid Hoffman, the cofounder of LinkedIn, had this to say about being an entrepreneur: "An entrepreneur is someone who will jump off a cliff and assemble an airplane on the way down."[8]

As Black women, we do it on half a wing and a prayer—with some chewing gum to hold it all together. We are notorious for making something out of nothing.

The First Three Years of Your Business

The early season or the first three years of building your dream business can be the toughest. Bouts of emotional struggle are just a part of the entrepreneur's journey. It's how you know what you're doing is worth it. You certainly won't know what you're doing for the first few years of business, and that's okay. The key is learning how to manage the early season through persistence, consistency, and good systems.

When I started, I didn't know what the hell I was doing. I had to learn how to fake the funk until it clicked. I was so used to working in a corporate setting where I didn't have to think about things like paying for health insurance, how much to take out for taxes, where to find clients,

---

8   Reid Hoffman, "Quotably Quotes," Goodreads, accessed November 27, 2022, https://www.goodreads.com/quotes/7962146-an-entrepreneur-is-someone-who-will-jump-off-a-cliff.

branding, logos, and so on. Learning how to do these things for myself as a business owner presented a steep learning curve.

I discovered the best learning emerges from trial and error. I had to be willing to lean into my curiosity and experiment within my business to discover what worked and what didn't. Doing so provided priceless information about where I needed to focus (what was working) and what I needed to change (what wasn't working). The moment I allowed myself to accept what I didn't know and gave myself permission to figure it out by trying and failing and improving each round, things started flowing better.

Talking to people who had been in my shoes and asking questions was key. I can't stress this enough. The first phase of your business is about figuring out quickly what you don't know. Be willing to learn and refine as you go along. If you see setbacks as irreversible failures instead of lessons, you miss the opportunity to turn them into your greatest breakthroughs.

A Dream Without a Plan is Just a Wish

The thing that trips us up when trying to follow a dream is the lack of planning. For many of us, having an idea is the easy part. Formulating a plan and sticking to it; that's the tricky part. Every dream, no matter how big or small, needs supportive structures in place to hold it up, such as productive habits, practices, and systems. Here's what I mean:

SET A DATE. Time-oriented goals are one of the most important parts of a plan. When you're serious about turning your side hustle or dream business into a reality, one of the best things you can do to make it happen is to give it a date. Whether it's a year from now, six months, or even next week, give yourself a date to get started. Having a realistic timeframe to work toward helps you stay on course. If you decide that one year from now you plan to launch your business, identify what you need to do between now and then to make it happen. Pick the date and work backwards.

Every year, get in the practice of writing down concrete career goals and target dates to make them more tangible. January is a good time to do this but really at any point during the year is an opportunity to set new goals or revisit old ones. Break down each goal into clear actions and give each one a deadline. Set reminders in your calendar or use a productivity tool to help stay on course. I remember at one point having hundreds of sticky notes all over my desk with random dates and notes—that was not cute. I got my life back when I started using Evernote, the productivity app to track all of my dates and to-do's.

But remember this: oftentimes, we put too much pressure on ourselves to make things happen according to an exact timeline, but this type of thinking sets us up for disappointment. Unforeseen factors can delay things. Life happens, and sometimes we get detoured, or we're tossed a curveball that throws off our timing. Know that we can always pivot and create new goal dates if we need more time than originally anticipated. Extend yourself grace, not added pressure.

Think of the goal date as your commitment to a timeline or a trajectory, not as a pass or fail. Let your chosen date serve as a structure for scheduling your time, not an alarm clock that indicates whether you win or lose.

ESTABLISH ROUTINES IN YOUR BUSINESS. Consistency is key to making progress. Without steady action, it's easy to lose focus or get distracted. Setting up routines helps build the discipline to prioritize business health and growth.

I have two sacred weekly routines that bring more structure and organization to my work. I refer to them as sacred practices because I treat them with the same reverence as a spiritual practice. Like the routine of going to church every Sunday, I bring the same practice of spending time within my business to connect more deeply with the work I'm doing by engaging in these two practices once every week.

1. *Goal Setting/Planning Sundays.* Every Sunday evening I block out sixty minutes on my calendar to set new goals and intentions for

the week ahead. This is my personal time to hone in on my focus for that week. I usually write out a task list including prospects to follow up with, people to network with, sales goals to hit, or any breakthrough actions that will propel the business forward. I recommend keeping your goal list small and manageable with around three to five items. This allows you to focus on only the most important items—the ones that will have the biggest impact.

2. *Reflection Fridays.* I block out another sixty minutes on the calendar to review my week. This is my check-in time to reflect on the highlights as well as the lowlights. I recommend using this time to celebrate any personal wins. If you made a sale, posted on social media, launched your website, or accomplished something—no matter how big or small—that moved you closer to your goals, this is the time to take stock. You can also use this time to note anything that didn't go so well, such as missed goals or a disappointing outcome. Next to each item, write what got in your way and ways to improve next time.

Consistency is key to setting up these routine practices. If you don't feel ready to stick with them for at least a month, don't start. But after just a month of the Friday/Sunday practice, you will want to keep going. Setting aside time to work on your business feeds it with constant positive energy. That's what makes this practice so sacred. It's like church for your business.

Are you ready to get started? Take out your calendar right now and mark off the next four Fridays and Sundays. Choose a consistent time for each practice. I personally use Google calendar to block out the time and not schedule anything that will conflict with it. I live and breathe by my calendar. If I don't put it in my calendar, it doesn't happen, so keeping things scheduled allows me to stay on track and manage my day.

Keep these Friday/Sunday appointments with yourself as faithfully as you would keep a doctor's appointment. Hopefully, you wouldn't skip a checkup with your doctor, so don't flake on your dreams either. Make this time with your business each week non-negotiable.

TELL ONLY YOUR CLOSE CREW. Once you have selected the date that you're going to make your business happen and you've got your Friday/Sunday time in your business consistently popping, tell your close crew, your cheerleaders. Your dreams will start to feel even more real when other people know your plans.

The caveat here is to make sure you choose people who will support you and encourage your dreams, whether it be a mentor, your best friend, or an online community. Think of people who will cheer you on, who want to see you succeed, and will kick your ass back in gear when you feel any doubt. If you tell someone who is negative or projects their fear onto you, you'll start to second guess the whole thing. This includes family and friends who can be well-meaning and well-intentioned but are caught up in their own doubts, so they'll try to talk you out of it. Sometimes people who've never tried to pursue their own dreams will try to tell you it's not possible to pursue yours. They can take several seats.

PUT YOURSELF OUT THERE. After you have taken those first steps as a founder and you start making progress, you will eventually need to put yourself out there and start marketing. When you're ready to start taking on real clients, it's time to tell the world about your new business! The moment you start creating results for your clients and customers, you'll want to start increasing your exposure and visibility. This a clear indication that you have an offer that works, and you don't want to keep that to yourself, especially when there are so many more people in your market that need that sweet, sweet solution that only you have.

Sign yourself up for your local chamber of commerce, go attend networking events, volunteer to speak at local community centers, write a blog, participate in panels, get interviewed on podcasts, or start one of your own! There are an insane number of ways to get out there and spread the word about your work and your business. How else will anyone know about you?

Going public can be scary and intimidating—especially if you consider yourself an introvert and would rather do literally anything else than drag yourself to a networking event and spit your elevator pitch all night. As a fellow introvert, I get it. Networking and trying not to come off as self-promotional was literally the hardest thing I had to do in my business. I had to make peace with the fact that networking is essential to making new connections, and that promoting oneself (when done tastefully) will be extremely effective at leading you to amazing opportunities.

Give yourself time and patience to build this muscle. If you struggle in these two areas, start working on it now. Hire a coach, get a mentor, use your full-time job to practice taking credit for your wins and promote your way into a new role or salary increase. The same tactic applies as business owner. Use every opportunity to hone this skill. We'll go more into strategies in later chapters.

REMEMBER, CLIENTS COME FROM THE MOST UNEXPECTED PLACES. In the beginning, I spent too much time poring over every detail on my website. I bought my domain name, signed up for a Squarespace account, and got to work! Obsessing over the size of the buttons, adding links, choosing the right fonts, colors, images, not to mention writing the text for each section, and getting the format painstakingly perfect: I thought that having a website was the single thing I needed to be considered "official." It's as if having a website somehow made my business more real. I thought it legitimized me and showed people how professional I was. Plus, with a website, I could put the actual link to my business on a business card—when people still used business cards. I actually thought that once I hit the "publish" button on my website, all the clients in the world would start pouring in.

No.

Don't put so much pressure on yourself. Any branding expert would agree, your website is one of the most important pieces of your business to bring in new clients. But the truth is, you have no idea where your clients will come from when you first start out. Your clients could come from social media, speaking engagements, word of mouth, referrals, or even from someone standing in line at the supermarket.

One of the most common pitfalls facing new entrepreneurs is the decision to spend time building the perfect website instead of going out there and attracting clients. It's part of the "until-I-haves" mentality. It's when you think, *Until I have the perfect website /LLC/office space/ (insert random business credential), I am not really official.*

Nothing could be further from the truth.

While having a digital presence is incredibly important, spending too much time on administrative busy work—like tinkering with your website—is time you could spend making yourself known, selling your products, and getting new clients. I would much rather see you spend 80 percent of your time networking, doing outreach to potential business prospects that lead to sales, honing your craft, than figuring out what font to put on your website. Who cares? Your customers will hire you for your ability to solve their problem, not for your brand colors.

I recommend that new entrepreneurs avoid spending a lot of time and money building a robust website; even a simple one-page website to start will do. As you begin to build a reputation of happy clients, *then* you can invest in growing your web presence.

The truth is, there are many ways that clients will find you. In the beginning, your time may be better spent firing off emails to your close network of family, friends, and colleagues, and building your business through your existing relationships. Cultivating new connections through networking can also go a long way. The lesson: pay close attention to how your clients are finding you and be open to the unexpected places they may come from.

SOMETIMES A BRIDGE JOB IS NECESSARY. I used to think that unless I was full time in my business, I wasn't a *real* entrepreneur. I've even heard other full-time founders claim they are the real deal just because they're full time.

Who made up that rule?

Whether you have a full-time job and run your business on the side or run it full time, you are an entrepreneur. Period. Unless you have access to a trust fund, or a partner with a high paying job, you'll likely have to work a full-time job while building your businesses. Many business owners who eventually went full time first started out part time. It makes financial sense to have a steady job while you work on growing the business. My first mistake when I went full time in my business was not having the support of a bridge job while building my company. A bridge job is any job that affords you time and money to build out your business. When I eventually got a bridge job, it relieved some financial stress. If business was slow one month, at least I knew I still had money coming in to pay the bills. Trust me, there's nothing like lying awake at night not knowing how you're going to pay for things. Again, don't put that kind of pressure on yourself and your business, most importantly your craft. Find an easy part time job that requires minimal effort or if you're quiet quitting in your full-time gig, you can direct those overtime hours toward growing your business at your own pace.

A net won't always appear when you decide to take the leap and do what you love. It can be unsettling to know that failure is an inevitable part of the journey and one you will visit many, many times. There is incredible growth on the other side of failure. Every uncomfortable situation I faced made me the person I am today.

Nigerian actress Yvonne Orjii made it big in the acting world through her role on the HBO hit, *Insecure*. But her life before that was a different story. In radio and TV interviews, Yvonne often talks about the time when she was a broke actor living in NYC, doing comedy stand-up shows, and working a temp job before she made it. On a night where she was hungry and couldn't afford a MetroCard to get home, she experienced feelings of defeat and self-doubt about her decision to pursue acting and comedy. Even after making it in show biz, she had experienced so much adversity that she started to question the very thing she most wanted to do. A Black woman who wakes up to her truth is unstoppable.

The ugly truth about taking the leap in business—or any endeavor for that matter—is that it includes risking failure, building something with no guarantees, and hoping it all somehow works out. This is the most powerful place to be when you take chances because you'll learn a hell of a lot about yourself that you never knew before. Even though you'll likely gain a few extra grey hairs in the process, you'll live to fight another day.

Building a company requires a combination of *trust* and *hustle*. This was one of the greatest pieces of advice I received from a good friend who was a few years ahead of me in business.

Want to hear the worst advice I've heard?

Leap and the net will appear.

The hell it does!

At least, it doesn't happen all the time or when you expect it to. Sometimes you're gonna fall right on your butt. But what I know for sure is that if our ancestors and elders did not take the leaps they did in the face of impossible odds, we would not be here.

Who are we to let fear get in the way of who we are destined to be?

Purpose to Practice

Budding entrepreneurs come in all shapes and sizes, and the approach to taking the leap will be different for everyone. Let's define what a leap would look like to you right now. Grab your journal and let's start:

1. **In two or three sentences, write down your business idea.** What do you offer? It doesn't have to be fully fleshed out right now, just write down all the pieces that feel clear to you at this moment. Resist the urge to figure out every single detail and how you're going to make it work. For now, just focus on the *what* (your vision), not the *how*. For example: *I would like to start an organic soap business using only natural, locally sourced ingredients. My soaps are perfect for people with sensitive skin. Eventually I want to sell my product at Target and major stores across the country.*

2. **Declare Your Leap.** Whether your leap means quitting your job to

take your side hustle full time or calling a local distributor to sell your soaps, your leap signifies that step that will take you to the next level in your dreams. It must be realistically accomplishable in three months. In one sentence, write down what your leap will be. Example: *I will go from only selling to my friends and family to launching a real website for my business. I will raise the prices of my services to help me get closer to replacing my full-time salary in my business.*

3. **Take out your calendar right now and mark three months from now.** Write "My big leap day!" Work backwards and get to work.

Chapter 3

F*CK FEAR

I AM WEIRDLY FASCINATED BY THE idea of fear. I mean, seriously, I have had long conversations about the complexities of fear, where it comes from, and how it shows up. It's one of my favorite topics to dissect. Why? Because fear is universal. Fear doesn't discriminate—no matter what your skin color, background, socio-economic status, or who your great-granddaddy was. If you are human, you have experienced fear. However, over the years I've learned that the fears I experience as a Black woman in the world, particularly at work, shows up quite differently than for my white counterparts.

I spent most of my career studying fear, what triggers it, and how it shows up for us. Fear has easily been the number one topic that comes up in client conversations. The moment we decide to pursue our dreams, our greatest fears come alive.

Here's the thing: Fear has been around since the dawn of time. Back in the days of earlier humans when we had to avoid getting eaten by tigers and face other potentially life-threatening events, we needed a warning system to tell us to run like hell in order to stay alive. This warning system lies in the brain, and it's called the amygdala. It's responsible for the *fight, flight,* or *freeze* responses to perceived threats. When the amygdala is triggered, high levels of stress hormones called cortisol flood the body and prepare us to fight off a bear, run from it, or freeze in sheer terror. The amygdala is the area of the brain that helped us to survive as a species all these years. Now, while we and the world around us have continued to evolve over the years, the amygdala has not. The amygdala still thinks that we're fighting off bears and tigers and other threats that existed thousands of years ago. It's the very reason why, if public speaking scares the crap out of you, you might break out in a cold sweat or feel faint whenever asked to present to a group. It's the reason hitting "go live" on Instagram feels hugely intimidating. It's also the reason why imposter syndrome, perfectionism, and fear of failure exist for so many of us, particularly as women of color.

At the same time, fear actually plays a vital role in keeping us alive and safe from danger. Fear is the reason we're not all just walking all willy-nilly in the streets without regard for oncoming traffic. Fear is the thing that jolts us back from the curb when a bus comes too close. We actually want fear hanging around so we can live long enough to soak up all the goodness this green earth's got to offer. But when we're about to walk on stage to deliver a talk to hundreds of people and that inner voice is like, *what if I'm not ready*, that's when we're gonna want fear to go take a seat somewhere . . . quietly.

Narratives of Fear

Fear is that tiny voice inside your brain that convinces you not to try, not to speak up, not to rock the boat—in other words, to play it safe. According to research professor and author Brené Brown,[9] fear runs two narratives:

1. Not good enough.

2. Who do you think you are?

The first narrative keeps you feeling small and hidden in your

---

9   Dr. Brené Brown, "Listening to Shame," filmed 2011, video, 20:22, https://www. ted.com/talks/brene_brown_listening_to_shame.

business. This kind of thinking has you believing what you have to offer is not good enough, that no one will ever buy what you're selling, and that you might as well give up. It's a real pain in the ass because it causes second-guessing at every turn.

The second narrative questions how you ever made it this far and tells you that you have everyone fooled. Hello, imposter syndrome! This narrative won't let you raise your fees, charge your worth, or otherwise believe that you are really qualified to be a business owner.

Fear does not want you to go beyond your comfort zone. In fact, it wants you to stay there. For how long? As long as humanly possible. As long as you are in your comfort zone, you are safe from rejection, judgment, embarrassment, shame, being stereotyped, and all the hard feelings we try to avoid on a daily basis.

Here is the best way I can describe fear: fear is like that overprotective parent who will do and say anything to keep you at home in your room where it's safe. Fear is that parent who wants to protect you from all the dangers waiting outside your door. I'm not a parent, but I *have* parents. The degree to which they or anyone else who loves me will go to protect me is above and beyond—fierce like a mama bear. Those who love so fiercely can be blinded by their own fear and project it onto others. So fear can actually be disguised as love.

One of the first conversations I had when I started my business was with my mother. As a Caribbean woman with strong opinions about having job security, you can imagine that conversation did not go so well. Naturally, she was afraid of the risk I was taking. To her, not having a steady paycheck to count on for paying bills every month was absolute insanity. I remember clear as day when I was still at my full-time job, standing in the parking lot on the phone with my mother, nervously telling her how I wanted to take my business full time. It was one of those hard days at work where all I wanted to do was quit and do what I really wanted to do: be a full-time business owner.

"What will you do for money, Ari?" she beseeched over the phone.

In my calmest voice, I told her, "I'll figure it out, Ma." But inside, I was freaking out. My fear was totally her fear. What *would* I do for money? How would I make this business thing work? Fear convinced me I would end up homeless on the street. I thought about the embarrassment and shame I'd endure if I failed. What would my friends and family think of me? All of my worst fears came to the surface the moment I decided to become a business owner.

Doing your own thing and having your own business is an amazing accomplishment. As the CEO, you get to establish a vision for your dreams and take action every day to see them actualized. At the same time, a tremendous amount of responsibility comes with overseeing the direction and operational pieces of your business. You're responsible for the salary you pay yourself and your staff, for paying your own health insurance and hiring the right employees, setting up the right systems for your business, and of course, paying taxes. When you were employed, 100 percent of this was managed by the company you worked for, so you never had to think about the cost of health insurance or how much money to put aside for taxes.

Making the shift can be really scary and overwhelming. It's a big reason why many of us are held back, and understandably so. There is a huge learning curve, but fortunately, we get to start a business in a world where a quick keyword search provides answers to our questions. Google and YouTube are excellent places to learn just about anything you want—and for free! Our parents and older generations never had access to such resources, so we can do more now than might have been possible during their time.

As I've always said if your dreams don't scare you, you're not dreaming big enough.

Many of us spend our lives avoiding fear rather than confronting it head on. Some of us spend an entire lifetime believing the stories we tell ourselves because it's safer to believe fear than to explore what's really possible. Sometimes we need our fear to be true in order to validate the things we already believe about ourselves.

If you believe you are not good enough, if there is a bone in your body that believes you are unworthy, trust me, you will always find a way to settle for less. You won't ask for more because you believe you don't deserve it. Many of us struggle to this day with lies we have been told about our value and worthiness, especially as Black women. The truth is, those internal messages playing on repeat in our minds are not our own. In many instances, they represent internalized white supremacist, capitalistic, antiblack, societal thinking that has existed for hundreds of years—long before we got here. Toxic internal messages our parents, grandparents, and great-grandparents struggled with and passed down to us. It's everywhere. We have to be conscious of how it shows up in our community and how we can begin to unlearn it.

Throughout my life, I was always known as "the quiet one." I rarely spoke up in meetings, except, perhaps to ask a question or run through a client report. I was afraid of my own voice. I questioned myself a lot and constantly worried about saying the wrong thing, making a mistake, or sounding foolish. To me, there was a lot more at stake. I spent a lot more time worrying about saying the *right* thing than actually saying *anything* at all. *Should I share my opinion here even though it disagrees with the rest of the team? What if my comment is wrong? Maybe I'd better not say anything, so I won't sound stupid.*

This went on throughout my twenties and my early thirties. I was too caught up in my own mental drama to actually get my voice out there. Being on the quieter side often meant being talked over by louder, more extroverted people whom I then believed were "more important" authority figures with "smarter" things to say than me. Often these authority figures were white men so there was definitely a racial component to the fears I held internally. So often these beliefs about speaking up and others were reinforced and caused me to hold back.

While upon first glance, I can appear shy and quiet, I truly enjoy interacting with people and speaking, but I am most comfortable connecting one-on-one rather than in group settings where I get drained. Classic introvert. I am more intentional with how and when I speak, and the way I process thoughts and ideas. But back then, I wasn't as self-aware. I just viewed my quietness as a defect that had to be fixed.

This belief was hard to break, and it followed me as I branched out as an entrepreneur. It took time and patience to transform my perceived flaw into a glowing strength. I talk more about the power of introverts later on in the book. Now, I wield my power of introversion as a secret weapon in a world that loves to hear itself talk. Turns out, introverts make amazingly powerful speakers, fantastic networkers, excellent listeners, empathetic humans, and they are most likely to enjoy quarantining in a pandemic.

What? No more agonizing small talk at the water cooler about my weekend or awkward happy hour socializing; we can all work from home?

Yes, please!

You Can't Outrun Fear

I've learned that fear is here to stay. We will never be completely fearless; like an annoying backseat driver, it will always be part of the journey. So instead of outrunning what terrifies us or avoiding it all together, we gotta learn how to walk with fear. It's about seeing fear as a travel companion that is along for the ride rather than something to avoid.

Did you know that fear and courage can coexist? It's possible that the things you are most afraid of can be the very things that excite you. When I was about three years into my business, New York University (NYU)—one of the top business schools in New York—hired me to give a twenty-minute talk on pursuing an untraditional career path to an audience of about twenty-five people. That's it, just twenty-five. It was a very small audience, but my fear volume turned up as though I'd been asked to present at the Super Bowl!

Like, what?

It was a topic that I knew one hundred percent, but fear kicked in and kicked my ass. For weeks leading up to the event, I walked around with a pit in my stomach; the anticipation of failing miserably almost killed me. A lot rode on my talk. If I did a great job, maybe they would hire me again in the future, and I could get new clients and leads. I could grow my impact. If I bombed, it would take a very long time to crawl out of that hole.

The night before I had to present, I was a bundle of nerves. I wished that I could reach into my stomach and pull out the knot that formed in there. I even thought about canceling or "calling out sick"—an excuse left over from my corporate days—anything to get away from the terror of being in front of people. I would have paid anything to get out of doing something so scary, but I knew that if I *didn't* do it, the fear of public speaking would continue to haunt me. I had spent so much of my life running away and holding back from sharing my voice because I was afraid. I lost so many moments not being my true, authentic self and giving into fear; I was tired, and I had had enough.

Finally, I sat down on the floor of my bedroom and meditated. I went completely quiet and listened to my inner fear. I tuned in to what was really bothering me and let my fear speak to me. I listened to fear about failing, sounding foolish, being embarrassed, and being the center of attention. I listened to fear about being criticized or judged. I don't know how long I sat on the floor in complete silence, but for the first time, something started to shift inside. The tightness in my belly began to soften. I put my hand over my stomach and my other hand over my heart and spoke directly to my fear. *I see you. I hear you. I know you are scared, but I am doing this with or without you.* Sometimes your feelings just need to be witnessed, to be seen and heard.

The next day, the time came for me to do my presentation. Sitting in an auditorium full of people, my name was called from the stage.

"And next we'll hear from Ariane."

As I walked toward the front of the room, the nerves were still tingling but the tightness in my belly and chest had vanished completely. It was show time. As I turned to the audience from the stage, I felt ease. I used the nervousness and channeled it into my talk.

"Good morning, everyone! I am so excited to be here with you today."

As the words left my mouth and I heard my own voice fill the room, the audience fell silent. They listened to me speak. As I glanced around the room to see faces smiling back at me, I immediately relaxed and went on with my talk. Twenty minutes in front of that room had felt more like twenty hours, but strangely, it was the most alive I'd felt in a long time. And I actually had fun.

As I walked off stage after my talk, I was greeted by swaths of people waiting to speak to me.

"Ariane, that was so great. I feel so much better knowing that I am on the right path."

"The stories you shared were so inspiring. I thought I was the only one, and I feel less alone now."

"Thank you."

Members of the audience shared their appreciation for my approach to a topic they had grappled so much with in their career. The very next day, I received an email from an event organizer who was in the NYU audience the night before. She was impressed with my topic and invited me to speak at an annual women in business summit. The opportunities kept coming after that.

I share this story not as a happy ending to a tale about conquering fear, but to show that sometimes, just listening to ourselves—even the scary parts—is often all we need to break through. Oftentimes, we want to push fear down, disown it, or flat out ignore it. This is possibly the worst thing we can do to manage fear. Whenever we ignore the fear rumbling inside, it flares up even stronger. Fear is our body's way of pointing out something that needs attention.

If you saw a child standing alone, crying, and afraid, would you just walk past and ignore them? I hope not! You would stop and ask, "What's the matter? What is your fear? What do you need right now?"

And then you'd listen.

Imagine if we did that for ourselves—if we actually listened to our fear with compassion so that we might know how to care for ourselves.

Fear and Confidence

We live in a world constantly bombarded by messaging that preys on fear. By now, we've all heard the advice that we just need to be more confident. We just have to ask for what we want. We just have to work harder. Google *confidence* and you're likely to find formulas, top ten lists, books, and seminars to turn you into the confident woman you always wanted to be.

Barf!

We're shown images of women—usually white—arms folded, in a power suit, sitting at the head of the boardroom while staring majestically into the camera as everyone behind her looks at her in awe. This, we're told, is what success looks like. And you know what? For a while, as someone chasing success, I ate it up.

The things that eat away at our confidence as Black women are not typically the same as those that impact people from other groups. Racism in the workplace and the constant fight to simply exist wears away our confidence over time. We internalize messages of "not good enough" and start believing that maybe they are true. When we are constantly overlooked, minimized, told to wait, and refused the same opportunities granted to others, we start to believe that we aren't worthy. We question our abilities.

Black and Latina women are more likely to struggle with imposter syndrome. According to LeanIn.org and McKinsey & Company, 45 percent of women of color have been the only person of their gender in corporate rooms.[10] The weight of being "the only" in most workplace settings is a heavy burden to carry, one that cannot just be resolved by images of power suits and affirmations.

Many of us have spent most of our lives chasing this elusive thing called confidence that people say we need more of, as if confident is something we can become with the flip of a switch. We are taught to act like men in order to be successful. And let's be honest: if you're a white

10   "The State of Black Women in Corporate America," report, *Lean In*, 2020, accessed January 16, 2023, https://leanin.org/research/state-of-black-women-in-corporate-america/introduction.

cisgender, hetero man in this country, the world is literally designed for you to never doubt yourself and almost ensure your success. In conversations with the smart, driven, professional women that I have coached throughout the years, I've discovered the ratio of women to men struggling with imposter syndrome is at least five to one—and even higher for women of color.

I used to do career coaching for students at tech bootcamp schools, and I distinctly remember working with a Latina woman whom I'll call Andrea. Andrea was an administrative assistant who took a course to become a certified Software Engineer. The course nearly kicked her ass, not because of the intensity of the program but because every day attending class she felt like a fish out of water.

Andrea was the only woman of color in her class. Andrea was also a single mom to five kids, living on unemployment at the time and had never taken a tech course in her life. It's hard not to feel alone and question your abilities when everyone around you seems to have it easier and be moving ahead much quicker. I watched as Andrea went through one of the hardest times of her career journey, almost quitting several times when the weight of her goals got to be too much. But she saw it through and didn't give up. Andrea not only earned her certification as a professional in the tech field, she now earns a six-figure salary, regularly speaks on women in tech panels and is committed to helping others through mentorship. Proud coach moment.

Andrea's story is not uncommon. Battling imposter syndrome can feel like an uphill battle. And oftentimes, the higher we go, the more we encounter these destructive stories about ourselves. Imposter syndrome is especially prevalent when embarking on something new. Like say, starting a new business!

In conversations with would-be business owners, I often hear things like, "I don't have time to start a business. I don't have the money right now. Maybe when I get my website and business cards, I'll start."

Sound familiar?

Ladies, stop. This is me, lovingly grabbing you by the shoulders, looking you straight in the eyes, and saying, "No more excuses!"

What are you waiting for?

We don't need to check any boxes. We don't need more confidence, nor do we need our flaws to be "fixed." Consider this your permission to quit waiting for the confidence to do something that scares you. I ask you to consider the radical notion that confidence was never something you lacked but rather a reminder of what you've always had. That *who* you *are* right now is actually a perfect place to start.

I spent nearly my entire adult life chasing down confidence, reading all the available self-help books, and constantly measuring myself in comparison to people, many of them white, who seemed to have an easier time making their way. Growing up in mostly white schools, I learned at a young age that if I could somehow present more white, I would get by.

As a Black woman with lighter skin tone, proximity to whiteness was very real for me. From the way I wore my hair to how I spoke, I shaped myself to fit in. The fear of being "too Black" is something I didn't want to be accused of. I'm not proud to write that. Colorism is a harsh reality in our community. Thinking about all of the time and joy I've lost by trying to be someone I'm not carries a heaviness that I still work hard on in therapy to heal.

When I was ten years old, my family moved from the Bronx to Long Island, New York. I went from living in one of the most diverse neighborhoods in New York City— filled with eclectic personalities, immigrants from all over the world, and all shades of Black and Brown—to the suburbs of predominantly white neighborhoods. I became acutely aware of my skin color and how *different* I was. I immediately began comparing myself to the other kids and became aware of what I didn't have and what I was not.

Game on.

I was determined to keep up with the cool kids from white, middle class families, and I knew what I needed to do. To combat the fear of not fitting in, I tried to surround myself with the "popular kids," who were usually girls with blonde hair and blue eyes, with names like "Crystal," "Christine," or "Kelly."

So many girls were named Crystal—at least three per classroom with different spellings! And there I was, a tall Black girl with an unusual name that didn't sound "Black."

Yeah, I fit in real well.

Nonetheless dressing like my classmates, talking like them, laughing at all their jokes, and making others feel comfortable—that was my survival strategy for acceptance. I tried fitting in with the Black kids at school—all 10 of us. But somehow, I still never felt fully welcome there either. I suspect it was because I didn't quite pass the test of being Black enough because of how I talked; apparently I sounded too "white." I couldn't win. So I spent most of middle school, junior high and high school trying to fit in but never really belonging.

Playing the fit-in game can be useful in younger years, but it wears thin as you get older—even when it is something you needed to do to survive.

Sometimes we don't realize that, even after becoming adults, the ten-year-old girl who struggles with "being good enough" is still inside of us. We live in a system that was perfectly designed to make us question ourselves from the start, a system that hopes we never find out how competent and qualified we really are. Because as long as we're chasing our tails trying to figure out how to be more confident, we're not out there building empires, calling out injustice, and loving ourselves just as we are.

The Confidence Barriers We Can't See

The sneaky thing about fear is that we can't always see when it gets in the way. Sometimes, fear can appear as a series of perfectly legitimate excuses for why we can't do something. Sometimes those excuses are perfectly valid, but oftentimes, they are just convenient little lies. We can't change what we can't see and that's exactly how fear has survived over the years. If we are unwilling to confront the things that hold us back, we remain imprisoned by our own making. When I was invited to write for The Muse—one of the largest online career development platforms—AND get paid for it, I nearly turned it down. At the time, I didn't think I was a "real writer" yet, and I damn sure didn't think I deserved to get paid to write. I don't know what I thought a real writer should look like, but it sure the hell wasn't me. I was convinced that in order to be taken seriously, I needed to have more bylines under my belt and accomplish more than just writing a blog. Plus, it was my first paid writing gig.

I had terrible imposter syndrome.

I am so glad that I pushed back on that voice and said *yes*. If I hadn't, I would have still been waiting for some magical person to tell me that I am a writer and that I have something to say.

Here are some of the top invisible confidence killers and what to do about them.

Shying away from self-promotion

Anxiety about self-promotion often comes from the conditioning we receive as little girls: don't be cocky, don't toot your own horn. We worry about people thinking we're all that or too full of ourselves. We tell ourselves that if we just keep our heads down, the work will speak for itself. And some of us are just naturally more private and not about putting our business out on Front Street. If this is you, I hear you, Sis! But if tech bros from Silicon Valley have put their picture front and center on an app, I think you can have the audacity to be a bit more braggadocious.

WHAT TO DO: Consider any judgments or beliefs you may have around self-promotion. What does it mean for you to own your accomplishments and share them with others? What proud results have you achieved in business that you do not bring up in conversation to avoid being self-promotional? How might being more visible help others who need to see and hear your story?

Questioning personal readiness

I often hear us ladies say they just need more experience, more training, more research, more experience, more information, a website, business cards, and so on, to feel more "legit."

More legit to whom?

Left to our own devices, we'll fill countless hours with more books, research, and webinars to feel "more qualified." But endless education just serves as an ongoing distraction. Black women are some of the most educated people in the world. We are armed with more advanceddegrees and certifications than any other segment of the population. We ain't playin' out here, but sometimes we *still* doubt our skills. In some instances, we may need additional training to advance our skills; but in other cases, relentless studying may simply reflect doubt sneaking in.

WHAT TO DO: Question the voice that says you're not ready and focus on what makes you prepared *right now*. What resources do you have available to you right now? This could include life experience, related volunteer work, skills developed by helping others—even if it was helping your family eat healthier through meal prep. Focus on the ways you are already ready, and go from there.

Boxing Ourselves in

As entrepreneurs, we look at what other key players in our industry are doing, and we try to emulate them. When we're just starting out, this is common. We need some examples to serve as points of reference. However, by following other people's creativity, we stifle our own. What may work for others will not necessarily work for us. We have to find our own way to stand out and dare to be different. Entrepreneurship is a great vehicle for creativity and authentic self-expression. People will buy from us based on what we bring to the table that no one else has.

WHAT TO DO: Ask questions. Where might you be putting yourself in a box? Are you doing something in your business because that's the way it's always been done? Are you doing free consultations even though you hate them? Are you on Twitter even though you're not sure what a Tweet is? Are you creating an online course because so-and-so six-figure-guru has one? Be honest with yourself. What activities are you doing even though they drain you?

It might be time to give those activities the boot and turn instead to business activities that light you up, even when no one else is doing them. *Especially* when no one else is doing them because that's when you can carve out your niche!

Comparing ourselves to others

I've seen it so many times—the trap of comparison. Social media is a major factor in this. As we scroll, we see other people crushing it in business, which then causes us to question our own progress. But in reality, social media presents the highlight reel, a curated stream of success that does not represent the whole picture, just the best parts. Every person who's reached a high level of success had a beginning and a middle in their journey that didn't look so glamorous. As long as we define ourselves by what others have achieved, we will always see ourselves as falling short.

WHAT TO DO: Define success on your own terms. Is it the number of followers you have? Or is it the value you bring to people? Is it consistently hitting your sales goals? Is it being able to pay for your dad's wellness visits? Is success being able to work from anywhere in the world? Your vision of success is personal and unique to you. Despite what you may see other people doing, you can stay focused by hitting your targets in your own meaningful way.

Hiding behind the work

Sometimes we can get too comfortable behind our laptops. It can be the best place to hide, especially those of us who work one-on-one with clients. Yet many of us just want to be recognized for our ideas and the work we do. Fear holds us back from taking up space or drops us into the habit of prioritizing the comfort of others—especially when we know our ideas might go against them. We must be willing to place ourselves in front of people and at the forefront of radical ideas. We must learn to speak up and speak out with truth and conviction about the problems we're here to solve. In doing so, we raise our visibility and become better known in our fields.

WHAT TO DO: Take inventory of the time you spend in your business. What percentage of the time are you working solo? How much time are you spending in front of the screen, scrolling your social media feed, updating your website (for the millionth time), or checking your inbox instead of spending face-to-face time with people? Take an honest account of how you might be hiding in your business and make it a point to balance it by getting out there and being with others.

When You Don't Feel Qualified

God is going to send you places you don't feel qualified to go. "God qualifies the CALLED!"[11] I reposted this quote by Mark Batterson on my Instagram once, and it got hundreds of likes, more than double any of my other posts at the time. Clearly it struck a chord with a lot of folks.

We all have intrinsic qualities that sometimes lie dormant until the moment we are forced to call on them.

We almost always feel uncertain about venturing into unknown territory, but the doubts are just a natural part of being human. We crave growth, but a big part of the growth process is getting ready for the thing we want to grow into. We must give ourselves permission to venture into unknown territory and the room to grow into spaces that at first seem too big. We won't know what greatness we're truly capable of until we allow ourselves to be great. While we may not believe we have

---

11   Mark Batterson, *The Circle Maker: Praying Circles around Your Biggest Dreams and Greatest Fears* (Grand Rapids: Zondervan, 2016).

what it takes for that next big step, consider the possibility that there is an untapped part of us that was born for it.

Granted, there will be times when we're just not hitting it and doubt just won't let us be great. It happens to the best of us. When my confidence takes a hit, it's usually because I'm spending way too much time on Instagram looking at what other people are doing. Then the comparison game starts. I've learned that when that happens, it's time to disconnect from social media, close the laptop, call up my business bestie, or go for a walk in nature. It's how I bring myself back through practices that ground me and reaffirm who I am.

Navigating Fear in Four Ways

My own process of navigating fear is not to avoid or go around it, but to go through it. It starts with having a willingness that takes shape in four ways:

1. **The willingness to identify when the voice of fear is talking.** (Think of an inner voice that is loud and obnoxious, obsessed with the worst-case scenario.)

2. **The willingness to challenge the story.** (How true is this story I'm telling myself?)

3. **The willingness to seek out an alternate perspective.** (What's another way to look at this? Who can help me see this another way?)

4. **The willingness to determine a forward-moving action.** (What can I do to work around this? What's a small step I can take to move forward?)

I go through this journey every single time fear tries to steer me away from my true path.

It's not about reaching pinnacle levels of fearlessness and being confident all the time. We are all human, and sometimes confidence takes a hit. That's just life. Fear will always keep us on our toes; in my opinion, it is a worthy opponent and one we need if we intend to better ourselves and become the fullness of whom we can be. Fear is nothing until we give it power. It doesn't get to control our lives. Acknowledging the presence of fear but acting in spite of it creates strength beyond measure. It's a mental challenge that prepares us for anything coming our way.

Purpose to Practice

What do you fear most when it comes to business? Write it out. Open a blank page in your journal and draw a line down the middle to create two columns.

In the first column, write down every fear or concern you have about your business right now—from running out of money to looking like a failure in front of your friends.

1. **In the second column, write down the action you would take IF that fear were to come true.** For example: *if I ran out of money, I could always get a job.* Fear becomes less scary when you find ways to resolve it.

2. **Practice the four ways of willingness this week.** What do you notice?

Chapter 4
MIND OVER MONEY

OFTENTIMES, I HEAR PEOPLE SAY, "I don't want to be rich. I just want to have enough to live comfortably." This always bothered me. Why is having just enough to get by the baseline to strive for? Does *just enough* allow you to invest in your favorite women-owned businesses? Does *just enough* allow you to take care of aging parents? Does being okay with *just enough* to get by create opportunities for yourself and others to thrive, not just survive? Our ancestors didn't fight for our freedom just for us to settle for crumbs, they want us to have the whole damn pie!

Survival has always been the psychological cornerstone to staying alive. As Black women we can be resourceful; we know how to survive with very little and can stretch a dollar around the block. To this day, my mother—who has a closet full of the most gorgeous designer pieces—always says, "I will not pay full price for clothes." When it comes to bargain shopping, she can spot a deal from a mile away.

Growing up, we weren't rich, but we made it work. My dad did case management and social work for the Legal Aid Society, a non-profit organization that helps give minorities and low-income groups access to legal representation. He then worked within the criminal justice system for several years at Rikers Island, a correctional facility in New York City. My mother worked as an IT telecom systems coordinator at a global media company in Manhattan. At one point, she even had a side hustle selling Avon for awhile that helped bring in extra cash every month. My parents, both intelligent and hardworking, had modest salaries back in the eighties, nineties and early aughts. We weren't poor, but we weren't swimming in a lot of money either. Yet we always managed to have everything we needed—food, clothing, and a roof over our heads. We lived in a three-bedroom apartment in the Bronx and paid only seven hundred dollars a month. This was back in the eighties; paying that little for rent is virtually unheard of today. But to two young working parents raising two kids, it felt more like seven grand a month.

Back then, seven hundred dollars was a lot of money, and we struggled at times. Looking back, as a child, I had no idea how difficult things really were. Every Christmas morning, we had toys underneath the tree. We spent summers on the beach in Jamaica visiting with my grandpa. Birthday parties were always filled with balloons, cake, and all my closest friends and family. My parents made sure my older brother and I never wanted for anything. They shielded us as best they could from some pretty dark times when money was in scarce supply. They were surviving and getting by with just enough. But to me, we had it all; we were rich!

I remember a few times we had to light candles because we didn't have enough to cover the electric bill. Other times, the house phone wouldn't stop ringing with incredibly persistent bill collectors. A few times, we ducked calls from the landlord when the rent was due, and we didn't have it. With my dad out of work for a period of time, my mother ultimately had to get a second job to help make ends meet. I hated seeing her come home exhausted from one job only to immediately turn around and go to the second job. But she never complained; she simply did what she felt she had to do at the time. Looking back, I understand that my parents made choices based on what they knew. They were facing their own pressure and money fears, so they did the best they could with the resources they had.

As I write this, it's the 50th anniversary of hip-hop. And while growing up in the Bronx, the birthplace of hip-hop, allowed me to take in a new era of music, art and culture, my neighborhood underwent its own reckoning. The eighties also marked a rise in drugs, crime, and violence in New York City, particularly the inner cities. Hearing gun shots, the local bodega being held up and having our apartment broken into were all things I experienced growing up. My parents did not want to raise my brother and me in a place we couldn't feel safe, so they packed us up and moved at the first chance they could.

Moving to the suburbs of Long Island was a mind trip. We went from a Bronx apartment in a gritty city to a baby blue ranch house with a white picket fence, a front AND back yard in a quiet neighborhood. My ten-year-old self was enamored by it all. It was also the first time I encountered the game of the "haves" and "have-nots."

Even though I was young, I saw how money, or the lack thereof, places families in distinct groups of class and status. In my young mind, living in Long Island in a house rather than an apartment meant that we were "doing good." We hit the lottery of life, and we were moving on up in the world. We had a house with a yard now!

Every now and then on weekends, my family would pack up the car and take us for long drives, exploring nearby places we hadn't been before. One day we drove around the area surrounding our neighborhood. As I looked out the car window, I saw huge, beautiful homes on sprawling landscapes.

These were no ordinary homes. They weren't like the modest three-bedroom ranch house we lived in. These were legit mini-mansions that sat on acres of well-manicured lawns—some with boats in their driveways, satellite dishes on the roofs, and in-ground pools. They all seemed so luxurious, like a fantasy. When we were in the Bronx, everyone was the same level of broke. But this was something else entirely. It was crazy to see that there were real people who lived this way. I wondered who they were and what their lives were like. How was it that they had so much? And why didn't we have what they had? Somehow, I believed that we were not like them. I sensed a separation between us and them that

I'm pretty sure was the point for many of the people who lived in these homes. Anyone who lived in such grandeur was different, and the kind of people who could afford that kind of life seemed unreachable to me.

It's been a long time since my childhood on Long Island, but throughout life, I continued to find myself in proximity to wealth and luxury. From the people I surrounded myself with to the people I dated and the neighborhoods I lived in, I could see how the "other side" lived. Even now, living in my Brooklyn apartment in gentrified Fort Greene with multimillion-dollar Brownstones on one side and government-run housing projects on the other, I often wonder how many young Black girls see the tale of two groups and wonder if they think about their potential to access wealth like I had at that age or if it feels too far out of reach.

How we think about money as adults is a direct manifestation of early encounters with money and the realities we saw as a child. Those money beliefs follow us into adulthood and directly influence our ability to make money, keep it, and grow it. Our early experiences with money likely determines our experience with it today. It becomes a cycle that, if not interrupted, repeats itself. Our thoughts about money become our feelings, which then determine our actions, which ultimately create our reality.

It's not just the money messages we learn in our childhood homes that impact us but what we absorb from the wider environment and society. We are immersed in a culture that values capitalism and the acquisition of things. Every day we're bombarded with messages that tell us we are lacking something—the latest pair of Jordans, a new Telfar bag, a bigger house. We are constantly chasing the next thing in order to keep up.

Long present systemic and institutional disparities add to this; they keep minority groups and communities economically disadvantaged, specifically as it relates to race and gender. There is no shortage of money empowerment books and self-help gurus teaching us how to budget, feeding us positive psychology money mantras and new beliefs around money to create more abundance. Trust me, I've read and tried them all. While some information is helpful—like creating better money habits—no amount of positive thinking and affirmations can simply wish these divisive systems away. But this moment in time calls us to confront social inequities, our deeper personal money issues, and generational financial trauma so that we can heal the areas that need our attention most.

The caveat is this: We have to be willing to confront our fear and the existing inequities around money in order to understand and effectively dismantle them. It starts by going back in time. We must look at our first encounters with money and how our past experiences created the beliefs we carry today.

Early Money Memories

My money beliefs began to form as I approached my teens and understood more how bills worked. No more of the wide-eyed innocence I once knew as a child, when money grew on trees, and toys just showed up for birthdays and Christmas. As I grew older and realized that my parents had shielded me from a lot of the struggles we faced, I learned that even though I had most of the material things I needed as a kid, life was still hard financially.

I became resentful around money. I resented how much we needed but didn't have enough growing up. I resented how unfair it was that some people had a lot of it and others just didn't, no matter how hard they worked. I resented the division and exclusivity money created in communities. I resented the arguments and conflict it created in my house. I resented my parents having to work so hard to get it. Some of these resentments are still true for me today as I witness the stark inequities that continue to impact women of color—Black women in particular.

My deepest beliefs convinced me that money represented conflict, struggle, and lack. It represented a constant chase for something that disappeared as soon as you had it in your hands, living from paycheck to paycheck. It's when your money is spent before it even hits your bank account because, like our friend and political activist Jimmy McMillan says, "the rent is too damn high".[12]

These beliefs—the story I told myself—ultimately shaped the money patterns I lived by as an adult. I fundamentally believed that when it came to money, there was simply never enough. And even more dangerous was money's direct tie to my self-worth. My confidence fluctuated around the amount of money in my checking account at any given time. On a good day when I knew I had money in the bank, I was happier, carefree, more creative, more able to relax, and have fun. As soon as my bank account dipped to an uncomfortably low number, my whole mood changed. I became withdrawn, afraid, and unsure of myself. I became less generous with my time and energy. I became so worried about money in the bank that each dollar was spent with worry and hesitation rather than ease and expansion.

When you're just starting out as an entrepreneur, every dollar counts. Some months will bring in less than others. It's just the nature of startups. But tying your confidence to a dollar amount that inevitably ebbs and flows is not only bad for your emotional health, your body becomes worn down by the stress over time. It's also bad for business.

Looking back to my twenties and early thirties, I can see how my earlier experiences with money sneakily followed me well into my adulthood. I subconsciously recreated the money challenges my younger self learned because it was the only way I knew how to relate to finances. My money story caused me to rack up thousands of dollars in credit card debt before even graduating college, and to accept whatever salary was offered to me without thinking to negotiate for more. I took on low paying gigs—even when it didn't serve me—and would avoid looking at my bank accounts for fear of being overdrawn or not having enough left to cover expenses. I couldn't face the thought of money, let alone talk about it.

My financial rock bottom came when I had to sell all of my belongings and leave my apartment after a breakup because I couldn't afford to

---

12   Activist Jimmy McMillan is founder of The Rent Is Too Damn High, a political party based in New York.

live there anymore. I had $2,000 to my name—nowhere near what I needed to survive for any length of time in New York City. Essentially homeless—something I never thought I would be as an educated woman in my thirties—I crashed on friends' couches for months and even had to stay with my parents for awhile until I could save up enough money. It was one of the darkest times of my life. My shitshow year, I like to call it. Yet looking back, that shitshow year was an incredibly healing time. I was forced to confront all of my choices that had led me there, face my demons, and learn to make better decisions. It even brought my dad and I closer together and healed old wounds. Thank God for friends and family, the angels who lifted me up when I needed it most. Otherwise, I do not know where I would be.

As I went through that trying time, I remember thinking: *I will never allow myself to be in such a financially vulnerable position ever again.* Like never, *ever* again. Never again would I allow the fear of money to paralyze me. I was tired of my own bullshit and committed to unlearning the money stories that held me back. I wanted to break the pattern of struggling with money and live my dreams with integrity.

Learning how to be better with money and rebuild my life started with a come-to-Jesus moment and just being honest with myself. It took time. I had to look squarely at my numbers without shame and create a plan. I had to learn how to show up consistently and work regularly at undoing my old money habits to create new ones. I had to get honest with the choices I was making—and not making—about money.

The truth was, as much as I wanted more money, my collection of subconscious beliefs kept me exactly where I was: broke. Simply put, I was in my comfort zone. Even though my situation caused pain and struggle, it was my comfort zone because it was easy to stay there. It's what I knew. Uprooting money challenges meant getting uncomfortable.

Take a moment to check in on the money stories you heard growing up. What statements did you hear the most?

Money Mindset

Sometimes, embarking on the entrepreneurial path brings our darkest money messages to the surface so that we have to deal with them. I had to work through the money story that I was hurting people by charging them. And not just people, women. Ninety-nine percent of the clients I worked with were women. No coincidence there.

I believe we are subconsciously drawn to help the people we most identify with because there is something inside us that needs to heal. The people we most relate to serve as mirrors reflecting parts of ourselves. When I was paid by my women clients, I believed I was literally taking food out of their mouths. I believed that by taking their money, I was leaving them with less. (I never felt this way with male clients.)

My clients represented every woman I saw growing up who experienced struggle and hardship. In many communities of color, struggle and survival are common. This is why I dedicated my career to serving and advancing Black women who are stuck in survival mode. I want better for us. What a beautiful paradox for the journey: the beliefs that imprison us are the gateways to our freedom.

Barbara (née Stanny) Huson, a financial educator and money empowerment teacher, defines underearning as making less than needed or desired despite efforts to do otherwise. However, Barbara leaves out an important point. The factors that contribute to underearning—particularly for women of color—largely stem from societal structures such as capitalism and economic inequalities that impact marginalized and underrepresented groups. More insidiously, underearning happens when a deeply rooted insecurity or low self-worth causes personal devaluation or replicated patterns of struggle and survival.

While a big part of our money story comes from childhood, a person's money mindset is just one piece of a much larger puzzle. Many of us come from ancestral lineages where surviving on very little was the norm. While it can be good to make the best use of whatever is available, it becomes problematic when you don't ask for more because you believe you don't deserve it or become comfortable with having less. Your mindset accommodates the financial threshold you are comfortable with. It makes choices aligning with that particular level of thinking. When you expand your financial threshold, your mindset expands toward choices accommodating growth.

Say you make $75,000 a year. How you view this number determines your experience of it. Every choice you make—from where you live to what grocery and retail stores you shop at—will reflect this number. Say you get a pay raise. Now you are making $100,000 a year. You'll likely "splurge" a bit more or make more expensive buying decisions. But even though you're making more money, you'll still feel like you don't have enough.

As we make more, we tend to spend more. We make less, we tend to spend less. It's money psychology.

If money was a person you were in a relationship with, how would you describe it? I used to describe money as elusive. Never around. Always running away. Tricky. Sneaky. Denier of fun. Deceitful and likely to betray. I also thought of it as something I wasn't worthy or deserving of.

Ironically, how I described money back then sounded a lot like the people I dated. Coincidence? Not really.

I learned that in many ways, the relationship we have with money mimics the relationship we have with others. If we give others the power to determine our happiness, if we allow others to mistreat us, and if we mistreat ourselves—if we don't value ourselves—why should we expect others to? If you have a hard time trusting people or trusting yourself, you likely will see that lack of trust show up in your money story as well.

The Money Practice that Changed My Life

In the early days of my business, money was scarce. There was no seed money from family and friends, no rich uncle with a stack of cash. I was afraid of taking on more debt, so business loans were out of the question. I made the hard decision to cut out extravagances; this meant more cooking at home, shopping at vintage and thrift stores, only purchasing half-priced happy hour drinks, and saving all the money I earned to reinvest in the business. But what I lacked in financial resources, I made up for by tapping into a healthy combination of faith and resourcefulness.

One day, I decided to take it a step further and get real about growing my money. I started a money practice that forever changed my life: Financial Fridays.

Financial Fridays are sacred money dates. Every Friday, I block out time between 9:00 and 11:00 a.m. and sit in front of my laptop to review my finances. I look at all my bank accounts, credit card statements, investments, cash coming in, cash going out, and upcoming expenses. I set new goals to pay off debt and increase my savings. I track my progress week over week. I signed up to Credit Karma so I could know my credit score and created a goal to increase it.

Since July 2018, I've practiced Financial Fridays, week over week, consistently. If I cannot make a Friday—which is rare—I make it up the following week and do a longer session. Working with my money is so important to me that I am unwilling to let myself off the hook or miss any sessions.

When something is important to you, you make time for it. This holds true for the people in your life, and the same goes for your money.

I end each Financial Friday session with a gratitude practice. I write ten things from the week that I am grateful for, and I begin each sentence with the words "I am so grateful that . . ." This is the most important part of the entire money practice. Gratitude creates an abundant state of mind. You feel that you have more than enough no matter what your bank account says. When you're in this state of mind, you realize that the free coffee you got from the barista or the metro card you found with twenty bucks on it is really the universe's way of showing you that wealth is all around you. It is flowing toward you constantly—once you start paying attention. I believe strongly in this sacred money practice. In the first two years, I was able to:

- Increase my credit score by over 200 points
- Pay off $15,000 in credit card debt
- Increase my business income by 30 percent
- Build up my savings account to create a cushy emergency fund

The way I relate to money completely changed just by learning to spend more time with it rather than avoiding it. Checking my accounts every week taught me how to confront my numbers to see what's coming in and what's going out. It showed me that numbers change from high to low, and I don't have to get emotionally attached to what that means about *me*. I began to see money as just math rather than something personal.

I learned a few things they don't teach you in school too. Any finance or budgeting book will tell you that you should save money. And you should! But even though stashing money in an account for years may keep it safe and secure, that money actually loses value over time. Money doesn't stand still. The stock market shows us this every day.

I strongly believe that money is energy; money flows *through* you, not *to* you. Money has a natural rhythm, and we are just the conduits to facilitate the exchange. Its movement is actually a vital part of growing it and keeping it. We can't hoard money and still expect to see it grow. We must be willing to let the *outflow* of money become a normal and even welcomed experience, whether that means paying bills or covering unexpected expenses. Similarly, allowing the *inflow* of money—even in small amounts and in unexpected ways—should also be a part of how we experience money in gratitude. Learning to let it go is just as vital as learning to receive it.

Often, we are fixated on predicting where money is coming from and when. We get a sense of security when we know that money will be directly deposited into our accounts on the first and fifteenth of every month. With entrepreneurship, we don't often have the luxury of predictability. That scares most people. It certainly scared me. But I had to make peace with that uncertainty and build certainty in other ways if

I was committed to making things work in my business. When money is low one month, it doesn't always mean it's going to stay like that. The next month's income could double or even triple. But not everyone has that level of risk tolerance. Depending on personal circumstances, we can't all afford not to have steady, predictable income. There's no shame in that. Whatever your risk tolerance is, that is your truth.

Does that mean you're only bound to a nine to five job with a regular paycheck? Not at all. It just means having to think more creatively about how to reduce uncertainty in your business through planning, diversifying your offerings, having customers pay upfront, or creating recurring income streams.

My confidence with money has grown exponentially just from taking the time to get to know and respect it. When you pay attention to money, you begin to understand your numbers not as the sole indicator of your worth and value but simply as data. When you know your data, you are more empowered to determine what to do about that data. Whether it be to make more money, take a vacation, invest it—you direct where you want your money to go, not the other way around. Once you really understand this, you'll realize that it's where your greatest power lies.

Melanin and Money

One year, I attended a Women Entrepreneurs NYC (WE NYC) mentoring session for new women business owners. The audience was about 98 percent Black women ranging from their late twenties to early sixties. To begin the session, we went around the room introducing ourselves and our businesses. Some had just started their businesses, and others had been at it for several years.

I listened as each woman spoke with such enthusiasm and pride about her company. It was a supportive room with great energy, as though we were all there to see each other succeed. I could tell that many of the women in the room had not previously attended an event with so many other women entrepreneurs cheering each other on. The energy was fantastic, so inspiring and supportive. We had each other's backs and generously offered resources, ideas, and feedback, openly and honestly.

When we got to the topic of money, the speaker, Karen Mitchell, a successful Black Caribbean entrepreneur who started and grew her business to seven figures despite a bankruptcy on her record, made an interesting comment.

"Many of us are out here not charging enough in our business. If you want to grow your business, do not treat it like a hobby. We must know our worth, charge for it, and get paid for our work."

The reaction from the crowd was audible. *Mm-hmm*s, snaps, and cheers acknowledged their agreement. The group had plenty to say too. Many of the ladies chimed in with comments about their frustrations concerning money.

The truth is, as brilliant, competent, creative, empowered, ambitious women, many of us are still afraid of money. We are still unsure how to ask for more money. We are still afraid to charge for our offerings and instead, give them away through steep discounts that don't cover the cost it takes to make the goods or provide the service. Another misstep around money is we don't hire help we need in our business because we'd rather do it on our own. We are afraid of running out of money. We are afraid of not having enough, afraid of losing it all, afraid of failing. We are afraid of our own desires to be rich and make loads of money because of how it sounds or that we feel it isn't spiritual to want money. Ironically, I find that sometimes this mentality shows up most prominently among helping professionals or in the wellness community (i.e. coaches, healers, energy workers, yoga teachers, counselors, non profit professionals, or otherwise mission-driven workers).

It's foolish to believe that money isn't important; sure, it's not everything, but unless crypto currency completely takes over, the dollar is still vital. You must remember that money is just a tool, and to the user, that tool can literally open doors to new opportunities and can help save this planet. Money in the right hands can rebuild communities, pay a living wage, and save lives. It's an investment in people, business, and commerce that can change our world. It can empower disenfranchised communities and provide possibilities. It can mean the difference between whether a woman stays with her abusive husband because she cannot afford to leave or has the freedom to walk away.

We can't be afraid of money. Not anymore.

If I asked who the wealthiest person in the world is, you might say Oprah, Warren Buffett, or Bill Gates. When doing research for this book, I wanted to create a current list of the richest Black women in the world. Often, we aren't aware of or exposed to people who look like us who also represent wealth and riches.

Of the women I found, I recognized half. I'm sharing their names to acknowledge the many unsung Black women millionaires and billionaires (with a *b*!) out there—not just Oprah—whom we can emulate. At the time of this writing, the richest Black and African women in the world are:

- Oprah Winfrey ($3.5 billion)
- Isabel dos Santos ($2 billion)
- Rihanna ($1.7 billion)
- Ngina Kenyatta ($1.5 billion)
- Folorunsho Alakija ($1 billion)
- Hajia Bola Shagaya ($959 million)
- Sheila Crump Johnson ($750 million)
- Janice Bryant Howroyd ($629 million)
- Beyonce ($420 million)[13]

I hope we normalize wealth as something not just reserved for rich white men. If we recognize the new diverse faces of wealth, we can create broader portrayals of prosperity.

Let's talk about the state of Black women and money for a moment. Black, Indigenous, and People of Color (BIPOC) face some of the biggest

---

13   Mary Afolarin, "Richest Black Women in the World 2023 – Forbes Top 10," RNN.NG, December 13, 2022, https://rnn.ng/richest-black-women-in-the-world/.

pay inequities and economic disparities compared to other groups. On average, Black women in the US earn sixty-four cents for every dollar earned by white men in 2020.[14] When it comes to wages earned, for the average Black woman to make as much as her white male counterpart, she'd have to work 263 extra days each year.[15] In 2016, the Pew Research Center reported that the median Black household income was $43,300, while the median white household income was $71,300.

Then COVID-19 happened. In only two months of shutdown, over three million claims had been filed for unemployment. Data shows that just 13 percent of Black people who were out of work from April to June received unemployment benefits, compared with 24 percent of white workers, 22 percent of Hispanic workers, and 18 percent of workers of other races, according to an analysis completed by Nyanya Browne and William Spriggs of Howard University.[16]

According to *Lean In*, Black women are nearly twice as likely as white men to say that they've been laid off, furloughed, or had their hours and/or pay reduced because of the pandemic.[17]

Black women are more likely to be essential workers and have to work outside the home. Many have had to risk their health each day of the pandemic, oftentimes for minimal pay.

Even before the pandemic, economic disparities were severe. Before

---

14 "Women of Color & The Wage Gap," The Center for American Progress, November 17, 2021, https://www.americanprogress.org/article/women-of-color-and-the-wage-gap/.

15 Matt Gonzales, "Black Women Must Work 263 Extra Days to Achieve White Men's Pay," The Society for Human Resource Management, September 20, 2022, https://www.shrm.org/resourcesandtools/hr-topics/behavioral-competencies/global-and-cultural-effectiveness/pages/bl https ack-women-must-work-263-extra-days-to-achieve-white-men%E2%80%99s-pay.aspx.

16 Jennifer Liu, "Just 13% of Black people out of work are getting unemployment benefits during the pandemic," CNBC Make It, September 1, 2020, https://www.cnbc.com/2020/09/01/just-13percent-of-black-people-out-of-work-get-pandemic-unemployment-benefits.html.

17 "Black women aren't paid fairly," report, *Lean In*, accessed March 19, 2023, https://leanin.org/data-about-the-gender-pay-gap-for-black-women#the-pay-gap.

the pandemic, it was reported that in the event of an emergency, 40 percent of Americans cannot get their hands on $400.[18] This statistic is even worse for women, particularly women of color. How haunting that many of us could not get our hands on cash when we really need it. The COVID-19 health crisis in America further devastated communities of color.

The 2020 election year was one of the most important, most revealing times in history. We saw how the previous administration threatened the working class and people on fixed incomes with losing their health benefits and access to life's basic necessities. We saw how the lower-to-middle-income population was sorely deprived of the same opportunities as those in higher income groups. We saw large gaps in net worth across different races. I am disheartened at how many young adults, even those well into their thirties and forties, continue to drown in mounting student loan debt. The poverty level rose while the one percent paid only peanuts in taxes. We saw how Black women struggle to match the earnings of white men. We struggle to obtain the capital funding that will allow us to start businesses. We want to start businesses, not just because we dream of entrepreneurship, but because doing so is key to our financial survival.

The resurgence of the Black Lives Matter movement in 2020 opened our eyes to what is truly happening in the most disenfranchised communities. Confronting this uncomfortable truth demands we do something about it. This moment is an opportunity of reckoning. It's a chance to make different choices about how we spend our money, reverse oppressive systems and structures, and take action that aligns with our beliefs and values.

I've often said that *now* is a great time to be a Black woman in business. The conversation is moving toward the support of Black-owned businesses and intentionally seeking opportunities to secure financial opportunities and generate Black wealth. It's time to reverse our thinking

---

18   Annie Nova, "Many Americans who can't afford a $400 emergency blame debt," CNBC, July 21, 2019, https://www.cnbc.com/2019/07/20/heres-why-so-many-americans-cant-handle-a-400-unexpected-expense.html.

around money to one of equitable distribution, empowerment, and worthiness. It's time to demand change of antiquated capitalistic systems that survived and grew stronger on the backs of generations of Black and brown people. It won't happen tomorrow, but we can take concrete, practical steps today to restore economic power and build a better, more humanistic system.

Purpose to Practice

1. **Ask yourself a few questions to begin unpacking and healing your money beliefs:**

    a. What was your first money memory?

    b. Where do you feel tension when it comes to money?

    c. If money was a person that you were in a relationship with, how would you describe that relationship? Loving? Conflicted? Stressful?

2. **Write a letter to money.** *Dear Money, I love you, but I am afraid of you. When you come around, I'm afraid you won't stay*, etc. This exercise is a powerful one, and you will start to see your money beliefs come through in an eye-opening way.

3. **Start your own Financial Friday money practice!** It can be Financial Friday, Savings Saturday, or Money Monday—whatever day you choose! Choose one day of the week to spend up to two hours on a money date. Set the day/time and do this weekly for at least three months. Use this time to review your bank account and transactions for the week, check your credit score, set money goals to pay off debt or increase your savings, and track your progress week over week. Let this be a fun exercise where you get to know your numbers and put them to work for you! Remember, when it comes to money, it's just math. Don't personalize it; use the info to know where you stand and make a plan for where you want to be.

Chapter 5

BUILD YOUR BRAND, BUILD A LEGACY

'VE ALWAYS BEEN KIND OF awkward. I grew from a cute, chubby baby with the drumstick thighs into a tall, thin, long-limbed girl throughout my teens and adolescent years. As the tallest in my class, I often got stuck in the back row at school. I didn't play basketball, so all that height seemed like a waste. I was so self-conscious of how I looked I would hide my skinny chicken legs inside baggy jeans—even in the summertime when it was hot. It was rough, y'all. I weighed like *no* pounds, so sometimes I would deliberately eat fatty foods to gain weight. Of course, that didn't work. I had such a block around my appearance that I would always try to hide or minimize myself in some way.

Many of us have been taught to hide what is different about us, especially the parts we are ashamed of—like my skinny teenage legs—to avoid standing out. In our society, anything that's not considered "normal," or a part of mainstream culture, is overlooked, undervalued, or straight out ignored. For years we have internalized this type of damaging messaging. We're made to feel ashamed about our natural gifts, abilities, and cultural identity. We downplay our unique characteristics by hiding them, or worse, assimilate to fit in. This is especially damaging to the voices of BIPOC (Black Indigenous People of Color) women and marginalized groups who have over the years been either erased or silenced.

I started a business in 2011 at the height of the modern-day women's movement. Everywhere I looked it was *girl boss* this and *lady boss* that; oh, and don't forget *fempreneur* and *SHE-O*. Ew. At first it was exciting and empowering to see women taking back our power and asserting feminine leadership. As a woman, I was excited to be a part of that narrative. As a queer, *Black* woman, I felt anything but. That's because the mainstream women's movement as it related to career, business, and leadership mostly reflected one group: straight, white women. Top selling business books were written by prominent voices in this group like Sheryl Sandberg (*Lean In*),[19] Sophia Amoruso (*#Girlboss*),[20] and Jen Sincero (the *You Are a Badass* series).[21] These were the top voices sharing their version of what it was like to be a badass woman in business. While in the last several years we've seen some advancements toward greater diversity that includes more stories of women of color, mainstream media still underrepresents business leaders who look like me. There still exists a certain default image that we think of when it comes to women's entrepreneurship.

Let's put that theory to the test. When I say, "Lexus," what comes to mind? You might think *luxury, fancy, high-end,* and perhaps recall those Christmas commercials of a Lexus sitting in a driveway with a big bow on the hood. (Seriously, who does that?)

What about "Hip Hop"? You might think of Jay-Z, Queen Latifah, MC Lyte, Tupac, Biggie, or some of your favorite rappers of the eighties, nineties, and early aughts.

And what does "Stacey Abrams" make you think of? *Leader, voting rights, Georgia, amazing, powerful, voice for the culture*—we can go on, but you get the point.

Now think about "tech entrepreneur," "venture capitalist," or "physician." Chances are, a Black woman in dreads with a Jamaican accent is

---

19   Sheryl Sandberg, *Lean In* (New York: Knopf, 1st edition, 2013).

20   Sophia Amoruso, *Girlboss* (New York: Penguin Random House, 2015).

21   Jen Sincero, *You Are a Badass* (New York: Running Press Adult, 1st edition, 2013).

not the first image that comes to mind. As Black women entrepreneurs, we have an incredible opportunity to step out from hiding and bring a new voice to industries that have been traditionally led by a white majority. By elevating our cultural identity as a key asset to the success of our business, it is no longer a liability.

It begins by building our personal brand from the inside, out. Understanding how to brand ourselves eventually leads to building our legacy.

What is a Brand?

When we think of brands, we tend to think of them in terms of business names, bios, what's on our résumés, our LinkedIn profiles, or the colors we use on packaging and websites. But this is only a small piece of who we are and the power we have to create an impact and build influence.

Some of us have never seen ourselves as an actual brand and haven't really considered how our brand affects our careers. As the CEO of your business, the brand of YOU is what brings value to the business, not what you produce. Think of yourself as the face of your business. Invest in yourself and serve the world with your unique ideas, strengths, gifts, and lived experiences. In short, you *are* the business. Read that last part again.

A personal brand brings together a unique set of ingredients that, when artfully blended, represents who you are, what you do, and how you lead. It's what makes you distinctive, relevant, and memorable.

You might be thinking, *But Ariane, I'm not a big company; why do I even need a brand?* In the ever-changing world of work, your brand stays with you wherever you go in your professional journey. As markets fluctuate and companies experience highs and lows, your brand is the one thing you will always have control over and the ability to (re)create again and again. Be unafraid to stand out amidst a sea of bland people who do the same thing as you do. Take the time to dig deep and carve out your unique brand identity. If you don't, you'll lose out on a true connection with an audience, customers, and clients who absolutely need what you do.

People want to do business with and buy from brands they can relate to, businesses that connect with their core values. If you are unclear about what that means for you, it's easy to get lost or swept up in an already crowded market. Don't let that happen to you. Your business is far stronger when built on a firm, well-branded foundation, rather than on loose ideas that blow away like sand with the slightest gust.

Googling *personal brand* draws a number of different definitions. Exactly what it is can be a bit nebulous. That's because the practice of building a personal brand really is a deep dive into self-(re)discovery. As multidimensional, creative beings, it can be difficult to distill our whole beingness into one cute package. So let's simplify how we talk about brand and define it according to these three things:

1. The unique set of ingredients that set you apart and allow you to stand out.

2. The experience of you and what people come to expect from you.

3. The value that ONLY YOU can bring to the table.

In short, it's your point of differentiation.

In the first few years of building my coaching practice, I spent way too much time looking at what other coaches were doing and how they branded themselves. I wasted so much time doing things that didn't make sense for me and my business instead of focusing on what I was already good at and what was unique to me.

To get clear on my brand, I had to discover my WHY. Why did I want to be a career coach? So often we focus on *what* we do rather than *why* we do it. Author and leadership expert, Simon Sinek this in his book, *Start with Why*. He says, "people don't buy what you do, they buy why you do it."[22]

---

22   Simon Sinek, *Start With Why: How Great leaders Inspire Everyone to Take Action* (New York: Penguin/Portfolio, 2011), 41.

I realized that I always worked in the career development space because I see our careers as portals toward freedom. It's the one place that we spend more than half our lives, yet endure so much stress and constriction. For Black folks, our first encounters with work stems from four hundred years of forced labor on plantations. Our ancestors were robbed of their freedom, their passions, their dreams, robbed of their sense of purpose and ability to earn a living wage to become self-sufficient. We've had to learn how to pave our own way and break free. Our careers serve as pathways towards the freedom we seek.

Same thing goes for the *why* behind my passion for entrepreneurship. I believe in entrepreneurship as a tool for greater freedom, creativity, impact, and wealth creation for communities of color.

I met a fellow Black woman entrepreneur at a networking event one year. Her elevator pitch was impeccable—I was truly blown away at how clearly she explained the *what* and the *how* of her company, a nail polish business that made chemical-free nail polish. Of course, she was wearing her own nail polish as she extended her hand to show me the colors of her new line. And yet, as I stood there with her, I couldn't help but feel something important was missing from her presentation.

Finally, I asked her what inspired her to create a nail polish business. What was the motivation behind the work that she was so clearly very passionate about? She shared that ever since she was little, her mother took pride in having her nails done with the most beautiful, bold colors. After her mother passed away, that image was one of the things she remembered most about her—and it inspired her to start a nail polish business.

Boom! There it was, the *why* behind her work.

Her story made such an impression on me, I went home that day and purchased a bottle of nail polish and told a few of my friends about my new purchase and why I loved it. THAT is the power of knowing your bigger *why* and how it impacts your brand story.

Knowing Your Why

Maybe the *why* for your business is clear for you. If it isn't, you'll need to spend some time clarifying it. But I guarantee that knowing your *why* will save you when your business goes through challenges or low points. Your *why* will be the thing that gets you out of bed every morning to fight another day. And most of all, your *why* will be the distinguishing factor that connects with your audience and turns them into raving fans. Your *why* contains your passion, purpose, and belief system. When you can articulate that in a clear and compelling way, you will connect with others who share your *why*.

The next thing you'll really need to get clear on are your strengths. These are the things you do so well and so naturally that you can do them in your sleep. What are those things for you? What are you really good at?

Sometimes, we tend to downplay our natural gifts because they come so easily to us that we don't think they're anything special, or we think anyone can do it. Wrong! I am the absolute worst when it comes to keeping the books in my business. Math? *Bleh*, no thank you! On the other hand, my accountant eats, breathes, and sleeps tax planning and truly enjoys working with numbers. But her excellent tax and accounting skills aside, one of the reasons I hired her was her empathetic and mindful approach to finances. She believes that doing your taxes doesn't have to be hard, and she brings simplicity into the process. Her ability to understand me as an entrepreneur and her approach to creating good money habits as something that starts from within was really refreshing. It's the reason I happily hire her every year during tax time.

When we consider our strengths and skills, we don't necessarily have to focus on just hard skills. These are specific abilities that are required to do a job like coding or bookkeeping. These are skills you often pick up through training or are learned over time. Our strengths can also include soft skills or personality traits as well. A lawyer with a sense of humor might find that skill comes in handy when working with clients on intense legal matters. An introvert may find their compassion and ability to listen a secret weapon. An ability to process ideas from a different perspective or think deeply about alternatives before arriving at a solution might give you an edge for creating great customer-centric products.

We all have unique capabilities, gifts, and natural strengths. How we bring them together and leverage them distinguishes us from one another. When we bring awareness to what we are really good at and what sets us apart, we have a distinct advantage. We can lead from a place of power. Embracing all the parts of ourselves, especially the parts we try to hide or downplay, is often the key to our success.

Putting together the key pieces of a personal brand requires going within to discover unique elements about ourselves. It also requires enlisting the help of friends and colleagues—people who can speak to us and our work to give meaningful feedback. Sometimes, other people can see us better than we see ourselves, and it's important to get a 360-degree view.

As I was going through this exercise myself, I attended a talk led by my colleague Jennefer Witter, who runs a public relations agency. She shared four questions everyone should ask their network when building their brand. Select five people total from both your personal circle and professional network and asking them the following:

1. In your own words, how would you describe me?

2. How would you describe what I do to someone you just met?

3. What do I excel at?

4. What can I do better?[23]

As you gather responses to these questions, you'll start to see patterns and themes. Compile the top common themes that resonate with you

---

23   Witter shared these questions publicly, but you can also find them in her book, *The Little Book of Big PR: 100+ Quick Tips to Get Your Small Business Noticed* (New York: AMACON, 2015).

and practice leaning into them; they will help define your personal brand. You might see themes centered around *creative, good connector, innovative*. How might you take your discoveries and leverage them?

Our Cultural Upbringing is an Asset

It was not an easy decision for my dear friend and colleague, Jessica Perilla of JPD Studio, to leave her employer and start her own company. Still, she was driven by a desire to create something of her own. When I interviewed Jessica about what it was like being a woman of color in tech, she recalled the pushback and challenges of being the only in one of the most male-dominated fields. "Being in meetings in a room full of tech engineers, I realized I needed to carve out spaces to speak and command attention. No one would look to me as the person running the meeting; they would look to the guys who obviously looked like techies."

As a minority woman in tech, she quickly learned her greatest business asset was not only being a woman, but also her heritage as a Latina. She runs her all-women firm with some of the biggest clients in the world, some of whom hired her in part because of her cultural identity and her values around supporting BIPOC women in tech.

Our connection to culture can be the driving force behind why we do what we do as business owners. If you were brought up in a household that viewed food as a love language or took pride in hard work, those values can be a powerful way to bring deeper connection to your *why* as it relates to the work you do. In a conversation with my mentor—a Black woman who speaks fluent Spanish and has roots in both Central Africa and Spain—she shared how often people would make insensitive remarks about her race and home country upon first meeting her. In these instances, she had to choose to either brush it off or educate others on their ignorant comments.

But the truth is, the fact that she is African born is one of the greatest pieces of her brand. In a world where representation matters, this piece of her identity amplifies her presence and impact as a leader to powerfully connect to an audience. Her cultural roots and international presence are assets for building influence and opening doors to projects and media channels that value her perspective.

Personally, as someone who identifies with Caribbean culture and being raised in that space, my personal stories and connection to the island makes me different. I love when I meet someone who is from Jamaica or knows the culture because that person can immediately relate to my experiences.

Sometimes society or traditional professional settings hold certain images or stereotypes that we don't question. By lifting up our culture as a valued piece of our identities, we can break through assumptions and create greater representation to our respective fields. For example, the wellness industry was long portrayed from the perspective of the dominant culture. It wasn't until practitioners of ancient practices from yoga to veganism brought their teachings to social media that many of us became aware of these sacred practices from Indigenous cultures.

Remember Our Names

So much of your brand has to do with what people think and feel when they see your name. Your name, whether it be on your LinkedIn profile, résumé, or your website URL, with diligent branding, has the power to evoke recognition of your reputation and the value you bring to the table. For years, Black women have been criticized and downright dismissed in the professional world because of our names. As recently as 2018, a St. Louis woman was rejected after applying to a customer service job. The employer had this to say: "Unfortunately, we do not consider candidates that have suggestive ghetto names."[24]

Creative naming inspired by pro-Black movements of the sixties and seventies gave rise to naming practices that veered away from common European sounding names. While the goal was to take pride in our heritage, what ensued was the inability of mass media and social

---

24   Elise Solé, "Woman says her job application was denied because her name is too 'ghetto,'" Yahoo! News, August 15th 2018, https://www.yahoo.com/news/woman-says-job-application-denied-name-ghetto-004856379.html.

entities to embrace our true identities. Black women have been made to feel ashamed of our names from our white peers and even those within our own race, calling people with Black-sounding names *foolish*.

In the personal branding world, our names hold weight; they represent our reputation, our heritage, and our legacy—in short, our name is quite literally, who we are. When you hear the name *Uzo Aduba*, you think Emmy-winning Nigerian actress. She tells her story of when she was a kid, asking her mother if she could go by the name "Zoe" because no one could pronounce her actual name. Uzo's mom responded, "If they can learn to say Tchaikovsky and Michelangelo and Dostoyevsky, they can learn to say Uzoamaka."

Don't Touch My Hair

I knew my hair was an asset the moment someone, another Black woman, recognized me from a few blocks away just by the way I wore my hair: big and free. She commented, "I saw the hair and immediately knew that was you."

In 2019, "The Crown Act" was created. This law bans any form of racial discrimination based on targeting hairstyles. Black women and even children had been told that our hair is "unruly" and therefore a distraction or not conducive to the workplace. Imagine being told that a part of who you are is seen by others as unacceptable or not appropriate. I once knew a woman who refrained from going natural and wore her hair straight because she feared the backlash at work. Corporate assimilation is real, y'all.

In the Black community, especially for women, hair is the centerpiece of identity. From natural curls and afro puffs to sew-in weaves and dreadlocks, our hair helps express who we are, and it shapes the narrative about what it means to be a Black woman.

In 2006, musician India Arie released, "I Am Not My Hair,"[25] an anthem to people everywhere (not just Black women), re-instilling pride

---

25   India Arie, R&B singer-songwriter, "I Am Not My Hair," by India Arie, Shannon Sanders, and Drew Ramsey November 15, 2005, Motown, digital release.

in our hair. The way we wear our hair is just a small piece of what makes us who we are. Even if we choose to go bald. In many ways, our hair is also how we make a statement, *our statement*.

Our work now is no longer about blending in but reclaiming who we always were and celebrating what makes us different. These are the keys to success.

Your Brand is Your Legacy

Let's talk about legacy for a minute. If you're building a business and a brand that creates a necessary change your community needs right now, you must also consider the legacy you want to leave behind. When you have a clear vision of a legacy that moves you and is bigger than just making a ton of money, each step along the way becomes about working in your truth and integrity. Every person you have ever met, every person you have yet to meet, every experience you've had—even the challenging ones—have, in some way, shaped or will shape your legacy.

The role you play in other people's lives is part of that legacy. Think about how you relate to others. Do your words build them up? Or do they cause divisiveness and pain? Do you speak the truth even when it is uncomfortable? Do you complain about the problems you see happening in your world, or do you do something about them? And most importantly, how do you treat others? Do you bring joy to people's lives? Are they better for having known you?

What do others say about you when you're not in the room? How do they talk about you? The way you treat people and their experience of you will almost certainly influence what others say about you when you're not around. If they are unclear or confused, it'll be much harder to think of you when they need your services.

Every challenge you endured, every proud moment that made you smile, all the chances you took or the opportunities you let pass by have helped build your legacy. Each move you make will significantly impact what lies in your future, and that goes for the relatively small things too. Every tweet, every Instagram post, every email, and every piece of creative work you've put out there, how you've led your team, the products you've sold—they are all integral to your legacy.

Let that sink in for a minute. It really puts things in perspective, doesn't it? When we consider how we've led our lives to this point and the type of human we've been, it becomes clear just how much our words, actions, and behavior have an impact.

Through her work as a poet, actress, and civil rights activist, the late Maya Angelou will be forever etched in our minds as a woman who stood for and fought against racial and economic oppression. Angelou's work remains some of the most influential of our time, and it continues to be celebrated around the world.

When we think of Angelou, we remember her regal, stoic presence. When she opened her mouth, she spoke unapologetically with passion and conviction. She was never hesitant to speak her mind. In the nineties, during one of her more memorable moments early in her career, Angelou came into a round table meeting of affirmative action leaders and said, "The first problem is you don't have women here of equal status. We need to correct this before you can correct the country."

Boom. Mic drop.

And let's not forget the notorious Ruth Bader Ginsberg, also known as RBG. The day I heard of her passing, I stopped in my tracks and yelled, "Noooo!" I don't know about you, but there are very few people in the world I don't know personally whose death could evoke that strong a reaction in me. Thousands of people from around the world held vigil on the day of her death. She committed her life to social justice and the eradication of sexism and political oppression against women. That is the impact and magnitude that her body of work, her legacy, left on the world—a deep void that was felt around the world.

When these prominent women died, the world went into deep mourning. We felt the pain of losing their light. We were saddened by the loss. Yet we will always be reminded of them because of their words, actions, and beliefs, and the way they chose to live and show up every single day of their lives.

Someone a little less known by the world but celebrated in her community was Ms. Thelma Lake, most affectionately known as "Tot." Tot was an exceptional lady. I first met her was when I was visiting my family in Florida. I noticed a tall, dark-skinned woman with vibrant silver hair and a glowing white smile. When she walked into the room, everyone took notice, and, like moths to a flame, they gravitated toward her. Her energy was warm and welcoming; she was poised and confident.

Tot was a caretaker of her community, both literally and figuratively. She worked as a nurse after she emigrated to the US from her home country of Jamaica. She dedicated her work to care for others through the healthcare system. In the words of her community and those who knew her best, she led by giving fair and equal treatment to all.

I remember Tot most from a special encounter during a New Year's Eve party. After a particularly tough year and a recent breakup, I was visiting with my family for the holidays. I sat at a table by myself while everyone around me danced in the New Year. Getting excited about the New Year was the last thing I wanted to do. Still, being around people beat sitting at home alone, feeling sorry for myself.

Tot must have noticed my isolation, because she made her way across the room to my table and extended her hand. "Come dance with me."

I looked at her pitifully and shook my head, but Tot was persistent. She bent down, looked me in the eye, and said, "You're never going to feel better if you sit around here moping. Let's dance!" She grabbed my hand, and I reluctantly followed her to the dance floor.

Before I knew it, I was smiling and laughing as we twirled around the dance floor. At that moment, I felt better. I forgot about my problems, I forgot about my sadness, and I was living again. Tot reminded me that, even in sorrow, we can always find joy again. A year later, Tot died of cancer.

Around the time of her death, I started thinking more deeply about legacy and the impact we have on those we leave behind. It's often only after someone dies that we remember the impact they had on us. The dictionary defines legacy as anything handed down from the past, as from an ancestor or predecessor. By that definition, it implies that legacy is something that originates from the past and is applied to the present. However, it falls short of the true potential we have right now to be intentional about the legacy we can design for our future and start building today.

I find it wildly fascinating that there is only one *me* and one *you* in the entire universe. There will never be another one of us in all of time. If that doesn't tell you that you are here to leave a mark, I don't know what will!

Doing Work that You Believe In

The grand beauty of cultivating a legacy is that, with constant intention, it becomes a living, breathing entity that continues to grow each and every day. As I've built my career over the years, I can see the ways my work has evolved and expanded, becoming more impactful with each iteration. Now, whenever I am offered an opportunity, I can quickly gauge whether it's the right fit based on whether it is aligned with my mission of empowering us to dream on purpose within our careers. A legacy serves as a touchstone to guide future generations. The concept of legacy probably hits home most for parents, as they often seek to pass their legacy onto their children. But I invite you to expand the thinking outside of the confines of your home and family life and into how you work and lead.

How does the legacy principle apply to the everyday lives of leaders, builders, creators, and makers?

It starts with doing work that you believe in. Whether you work for a company, or you run your own business, you absolutely *must* believe in the product you're selling. If you're an actor or in the film industry, get involved with scripts that enrich humanity. If you're a musician, dare to make music that heals instead of imitating what's trending in the charts. Create art that influences lives and makes a statement. If politics or government work is your desire, become part of a system that builds a society that actually puts people first.

Your cause or mission must be something you believe in and stand for. It must be something that you care so strongly about that your blood boils when you see its opposite. Such a mission gives you purpose. It's something you would fight for and devote your life to, even if it means losing everything, including the popularity vote.

Building a legacy requires taking risks. Building a legacy takes courage. There's no perfect time to start. Poet Amanda Gorman blew us away as the youngest poet laureate to speak at a President's inauguration when she was just twenty-three years old. Greta Thunberg, a climate change activist, began her journey at age fifteen. Emma Thomas, a teen advocate for gun control, launched a national movement and advocacy group in response to the high school shooting killing seventeen students in Parkland, Florida.

If you were born a few decades before these young go-getters, you might be thinking, *They started so young, and they still have their whole lives ahead of them to build their legacies; it's too late for me.* To that, I say—in the famous words of the late R&B singer Aaliyah—"age ain't nothin' but a number." Ava DuVernay took the leap into film after first picking up the camera at thirty-three. She debuted her first documentary at age thirty-five, and then went on to direct the powerful film *Selma* at age forty-two. Leslie Jones, the hilarious comedian and actress, hit fame at age forty-seven when she landed a spot as a recurring cast member on Saturday Night Live.

There's never been a more perfect time than right now to decide the impact you want your life to make. Time will pass anyway, so you might as well use it to build something great.

Building a legacy includes these elements:

- It speaks to a cause or mission greater than yourself.
- It impacts a specific group of people or interests.
- It is rooted in a core value that is non-negotiable.
- It can be taught to others.
- It must outlive you.

Let's unpack each of these elements using Tarana Burke, founder of the Me Too movement, as the example.

In 2006, forty-four-year-old Tarana Burke used #metoo to raise awareness of the pervasiveness of sexual assault in society. Despite a lack of social media presence, she used her platform and career to work with survivors of sexual abuse and sexual violence to raise awareness about social justice and gender equity. Her passion and commitment came from surviving sexual abuse as a child, and she used her experience to improve the lives of other girls who have undergone extreme hardships. Tarana said, "If we don't center the lives of marginalized people, we're doing the wrong work."[26] She didn't focus on her own hardships; she worked to raise the voices of those who are often silenced.

The success of Tarana's Me Too movement grew rapidly. It was built on empathy for others, empathy for those who have lived in shame and silence. Me Too removes the isolation. It makes it okay to be vulnerable enough to share our stories as a form of solidarity and unity against oppressive paradigms. Tarana's work helps improve policies in schools, workplaces, rape crisis centers, and more, through various programs. She helps victims reject self-blame for sexual violence. This important work and the millions of lives already impacted by her message of esteem, empowerment, and equity will continue for years and years to come. This is what it means to build a legacy that lasts.

Building a legacy isn't only for the Oprahs of the world; it's for regular folks too, like you and me. Since we are already walking, living, and breathing legacies that evolve every minute of the day, let's go from passively living out our legacies to building them with intention.

Start With Your Mission Statement

Building a legacy begins with crafting a mission statement that will guide your day-to-day actions and decisions, as well as your long-term

---

26   Emanuella Grinberg, "The next step for #MeToo creator isn't a hashtag," CNN, Updated 1:58 PM EST, Fri November 10, 2017, https://www.cnn.com/2017/11/10/us/tarana-burke-metoo-whats-next.

goals. Keep it simple, clear, and relatively brief—from a few sentences to a couple of paragraphs. How you craft it is less important than what you want to express. Try to keep your words positive and affirmative. Focus on what you want rather than what you don't want. When you have it, post it where you'll see it every day, where it can serve as a reminder for the work and the dreams you set out to achieve.

Writing a mission statement requires deep soul searching, so take your time and don't worry about getting it right or perfect on the first try. Your mission statement isn't something you do in a day. It requires introspection, self-analysis, clarity of mind, and often several drafts before you produce it in a final form. It might take several weeks or even months before you feel really comfortable with your mission statement before you feel it is a complete and concise expression of your innermost values and directions. Your mission statement is not set in stone; it will grow and evolve as you do over time. Consider doing a mission statement practice once every three to five years. This statement will serve you as a guiding mantra when it comes to your career path, the growth of your business, as well as the guide toward following your dreams. In times of crisis or indecision, your mission statement will become a North Star.

Here are a couple of examples of real mission statements from my clients:

> *My purpose on this planet is to make people feel welcome, to support and lift them up, and create a more hopeful and inspired world. I want to build family and a home that includes my children and husband but also my business and community. Inside this business and home everyone is welcome and seen for who they are. Surrounding this home and business, we care for the plants and animals, we reforest, improve the soil, and we make a sustainable life for all the people who come there—living in harmony with the natural world. We lift people up for who they are—regardless of their gender and any other preconceived ideas—so they feel free and strong.*

My mission is to start each day grateful for it having arrived. I will listen to what others are saying, and treat them warmly, with dignity. I will make time for my family. I will approach each task with mindfulness, and craft work that helps my clients thrive. I will tell my people how much I love them. I will always be striving for ways to improve on myself. I will forgive myself, work hard, and have fun doing life.

Envision Your Funeral

The following exercise was inspired by Stephen Covey's work around developing personal mission statements. While it might be uncomfortable to do, envisioning your funeral is one of the best ways to take charge of your life and minimize regret. Think about how you would like the important people in your life to remember you and talk about you. What would you like each of them to say about you and the life you led? What kind of person would you like to have been known for? What kind of work did you put out into the world? What contributions, what achievements would you want them to remember? What difference would you like to have made in their lives? How did you leave this world a better place?

Determining Your Earthly Assignment

You can think of this through the context of your business or the work you feel called or aspire to do. Some guiding questions for you to consider are:

- What do you believe you are being called into right now?
- How do you most want to express yourself?
- What is worth going for even if you fail?
- What idea/cause do you believe in so strongly that you wish everyone and your loved ones could experience (i.e., financial empowerment,

personal fulfillment/happiness, innovative technology, etc.)?

- What societal problem or human condition causes you anger/ sadness/frustration (i.e., food insecurity, lack of diversity in leadership, financial illiteracy, etc.)?

- What is the result you hope to achieve through your work? Be as specific as you can (i.e., raising the number of Black women lawyers).

- What are some action words that describe what you do or aspire to do? For example, empower, educate/teach, inspire, mobilize, enlighten, uplift, confront, etc. Circle the top three.

Purpose to Practice

1. **Make a list of all of your personal and professional talents, aptitudes, and skills**—even those you may take for granted like being a good listener or people connector. What are your natural talents? What have others told you you're good at? Circle the skills you enjoy or find fulfilling. For each one you circled, write out why this attribute would be valuable to your business.

2. **Ask up to five (no less than three) of your connections for feedback on you.** Pick people who know you well and have experienced working with you; pick three professional contacts and two personal ones. Ask each of them what three words or phrases they would use to describe you. Look for common themes and patterns in their responses. Highlight the ones you most resonate with.

3. **Write your own mission statement.** Keep it simple, clear, and relatively brief—from a few sentences to a couple of paragraphs. Incorporate the skills, the feedback you received from the above exercises, and all that is important to you. When you have it, post it somewhere where you'll see it every day to serve as a reminder

for the work and the dreams you set out to achieve.

Chapter 6
THIS IS HOW WE MARKET

A**S A WOMAN IN HER** late forties, my aunt one day decided to teach herself how to make organically scented candles. She fell in love with her passion and ultimately, she started her own candle business. In just a short time, she is now soaring as a business owner and sells out her inventory every time at trade shows. I'm just so damn proud of her. Yet, as someone with parents of an older generation, I wondered about the messages she heard as a kid growing up and how much of it shows up in her business today. One afternoon, over lunch in a cute little Brooklyn diner, I leaned over to ask her if, as a child, she had ever heard the old adage, "Children should be seen and not heard."

Her eyes told me everything I needed to know. As if she was immediately brought back in time, she was filled with the memories of adults and authority figures reminding her that children are to be silent unless spoken to while in the presence of adults.

"Oh, Ari, it's all I heard every day growing up in Jamaica," she said.

"You ever think that saying is part of the reason why we as adult Black women often struggle to speak up?" I asked her.

My aunt agreed wholeheartedly and also told me that she believed it's why marketing and bringing visibility to her business is often very difficult to do.

What we have been told as kids inevitably becomes part of who we are as adults. And if you happen to be a woman in your late thirties, forties (present!), fifties, or sixties, it's likely that you've heard the sentiment about being seen but not heard. Some part of you may still even believe it.

This thinking often shows up when it comes to speaking up and advocating for ourselves. When it comes to marketing effectively, it is directly tied to our level of comfort with stepping out and promoting ourselves confidently.

Marketing is defined as the activities a company undertakes to promote products or services. The operative word: *promote*. It's how we get clients and customers to buy from us. If we're shy about promotion, people won't know who we are. When people don't know who we are, they can't buy from us. And when they can't buy from us, they won't get to experience our amazing products or services—even if those very items could improve their lives. Can you imagine if Issa Rae was shy about promoting her TV series to HBO? Where would we all be without *Insecure*?

And here's the rub: if clients don't experience our amazing offerings, we can't make the money we need to stay afloat, to grow our teams, or take our lovers out for nice dinners. Our businesses deserve that, our lovers deserve that, the world deserves that, and most of all, WE deserve that.

Seen and Not Heard

Shyness is learned. If you struggle with speaking up due to shyness, it can likely be tied to what you learned growing up. Let's unpack the idea that "Children should be seen and not heard" a little further. In West Indian cultures, a child who can quietly sit still, listen, and be helpful to adults is considered worthy of praise. Parents whose children are obedient and well behaved are regarded as good parents with perfect kids. And that's the goal, to raise perfect kids. To be clear, perfect kids are the ones who don't talk back, who say *please* and *thank you*, are well-kept and dressed in freshly pressed clothes, and, most of all, can sit quietly while the adults talk.

In most households, "seen and not heard" *rules*. It establishes authority and discipline between parent and child so that the child always remains submissive to the parent. Rule breaking is grounds for punishment. Never was this made clearer for me then on Sundays at church. Through two-hour sermons (you know how long things can go at Black churches), the other kids and I were expected to sit completely still and well behaved without cracking a peep. We were about seven or eight years old at the time, and if we would so much as let out a snicker or wiggle in our chairs, my grandmother would give us "the look." As kids, we knew exactly what "the look" meant—and it was all it took to put us back in our place.

On one particular Sunday morning at church—it had to be Easter because the ladies around us were dressed to the nines, donning their best Easter Sunday hats—I was squirming in my seat after an especially long sermon. Bored out of my mind, I started playing with my cousin next to me, then we both started to snicker. My grandmother saw us messing around, and the stern look on her face said, *Wait until we get home.* The smiles were immediately wiped from our face.

As adults, we often look back and joke about those times at family get togethers. That one look from Grandma brought a world of hurt as a kid. It was the same kind of iron-fisted discipline that she received from her parents as a child and likely her parents received from their parents and so on. But it goes deeper. It's a painful reminder of the power structures that existed during slavery, where children were seen as property to buy and sell. Their value was based on behavior, not voices. Good behavior and obedience were a means for survival.

Coming from our history, it is no wonder that many Black women often struggle to see the value of our voices and to express ourselves freely. Being nice and agreeable are deemed as praiseworthy traits, particularly in the workplace. Similarly, when it comes to marketing, we may be hesitant to put our true selves out there for fear that we will appear anything but "professional." So we try to control how we look and aim for perfection instead of allowing ourselves the space to be vulnerable.

I can see now how this mindset played out in my career. Having respect for those in authority, even as an adult, sometimes meant being submissive and taking up as little space as possible around my managers and coworkers. Even now as a business owner, sometimes the good little girl part of me—the one who wants to hide—still creeps in from time to time.

So many of us walk around with this kind of mindset, hoping that if we just keep our heads down and work really hard, we'll be noticed for our value and efforts. But acknowledgement and validation often require speaking up and being seen. That makes us nervous. It's a struggle for a lot of us—especially if we are more on the private side or are introverted—and learning to become more visible can be an uphill battle.

Stop Hiding

Stop hiding behind your business. That's right, I'm calling you out! It's easy to spend so much time behind our laptops thinking about marketing that we never get around to actually doing it. Sometimes it's not even a laptop we hide behind. It can be any excuse or situation: indecision about whether to market on Facebook or Instagram, not having the "right" microphone to start that podcast, or not having enough time because of "busyness." These things often hold us back. Sometimes it's easier and more comfortable to be an observer or hope that someone will just happen upon our website and discover us. We work hard in our business and hope the results will speak for themselves. That kind of thinking won't work here.

With so many systemic barriers already stacked against us, we can't let inner barriers get the better of us. Ain't nobody got time for that! Any market in any industry will benefit from owner visibility. It's essential to let others see us and connect with what we have to say and become recognizable players in our fields.

Over time, I've added more marketing strategies to my rotation, but in the beginning, blogging was my main form of marketing. Blogging eventually led to getting picked up by other outlets with larger audiences.

Eventually, I started to get paid to write—imagine that! One year, one of my articles was published on the blog, Live in the Grey, and then got picked up and republished on the *TIME* website.[27] *The TIME*, as in the same company that does the person of the year features, published one of *my* articles? The way I called my mama so fast when I got the news. It was one of the first times I realized that this writing thing was actually panning out and would open doors for me and my business. After nine years of writing in my business, I was offered a publishing deal that allowed me to write the book you have in your hands right now. Look at God!

We can never predict the path our business will take when we begin, but when purpose is bigger than fear, nothing can hold us back.

Whenever I teach marketing, like clockwork, someone in the audience will say, "Ariane, this putting yourself out there talk is fine and all, but I'm an introvert and it's really difficult for me to be in front of people."

Whenever someone blames being an introvert for their marketing struggle, I smile. As if introversion is a personal defect that you have to live with. Girl, *nooo!* You have been given a secret weapon; you just haven't tapped into it yet!

Introverts Make the Best Marketers

Some of the most successful entrepreneurs are introverts. Most of my circle of business besties are introverts, and they are some of the best in their industry. My own mentor is an introvert, yet she is also an international speaker, constantly appears on global TV outlets, is on stages all around the world, and has even been featured in *Vogue* magazine. Sometimes those who are regularly in the spot light are the most introverted! In a recent study, analysts spent ten years examining the personalities of 2,000 CEOs. Guess what they found? The majority of

27   Ariane Hunter, "Escaping the Career Waiting Trap," *Live in the Grey* (blog), January 15, 2015, https://www.liveinthegrey.com/escaping-career-waiting-trap.html. The article was also published online by *Time* but was credited to *Live in the Grey* rather than Ariane. https://time.com/3702132/escaping-career-waiting-trap/.

successful CEOs were introverts. There is nothing that suggests extroverts have it easier than introverts when it comes to entrepreneurship. It's about the choices made, leadership, and getting things done. It's also about recognizing strengths and using them to your advantage.

As an introvert, you likely hate trivial small talk and are amazing at having deeper, more meaningful conversations with people. If you hate pretentious networking events, don't go! There are hundreds of ways to promote a business that don't include throwing yourself in large crowds that will drain your energy. Instead, focus on the activities you find most comfortable and energizing like one-on-one meetings.

If you hate speaking publicly, but you know it's critical to elevating your business and brand, take a public speaking class. I signed up to my local Toastmasters chapter to practice my public speaking because I knew it was an area I had to develop.

Introversion and shyness are usually lumped into the same category. It's important to distinguish the two. Shyness comes from a fear of negative judgment and is a mild form of social anxiety, whereas introversion is the tendency to become overstimulated without breaks. Introverts often need time alone to recharge or replenish our energy. Shyness is associated with a fear; introversion is associated with our energy source. Extroverts can still be shy, and introverts can be outgoing. Although we can't just be looped into one category, and other factors come into play depending on the scenario, this chart developed by mental health expert, Arlin Cuncic and featured on *Verywell Mind,* shows how introverts and extroverts might respond in typical scenarios. With her permission, I share an adapted version of the table on the next page.[28]

---

28   Arlin Cuncic, *"Introversion and Shyness Explained," Verywell Mind, July 25, 2020, https://www.verywellmind.com/introversion-and-shyness-explained-3024882. Used with permission.*

At a group meeting

Shy-Introvert	Outgoing-Introvert
I really do not enjoy meetings. It's very difficult for me to listen to everyone talking about their ideas without feeling self-conscious. I'm so nervous that I can't even follow everything being said. I'd rather just sit this one out and hide.	I enjoy being with people, but I get tired after being in a lot of meetings. Thinking before I speak is how I interact and that's hard to do live in a meeting. I like to take notes and then follow up once I've had a chance to process what was shared.
Shy-Extrovert	**Outgoing-Extrovert**
While I enjoy in person meetings, I tend to get nervous to share my ideas out loud in a group. Sharing in one-on-one settings is more my speed.	I love being in person and talking through ideas in meetings and collaborative exchanges. I do a good share of the talking.

At a large networking event

Shy-Introvert	Outgoing-Introvert
There is nothing more unenjoyable then being in a room full of people. I'm too nervous to talk to anyone. It's so exhausting and I wish I could just go home.	Getting to know people one-on-one is what I prefer. Being in crowds of people is very overwhelming for me.
Shy-Extrovert	**Outgoing-Extrovert**
I love being surrounded by people, but I'm anxious to talk with all of them. Speaking with a few people instead of everyone works best for me.	This is my happy place. I can't wait to make my rounds with everyone here. I get so energized in this setting.

Introversion is not the problem here; fear and judgment anxiety are.

In a conversation with my sister-friend, Joy*, who is from the Dominican Republic, she recalls what her mother used tell her when she was growing up: "Don't give anyone a reason to judge you."

Can you relate? Now imagine for a minute going through life trying desperately to avoid judgment and worrying about what other people will think of you. It's a reality all too many of us experience.

I worked with one woman who had spent her entire career as a publicist helping other women get more press for their businesses. She put it this way: "I just preferred to work behind the scenes." She got pretty comfortable pushing forward the voices of others while holding back her own. That changed the day she decided it was time to step out and give her own voice the spotlight as an entrepreneur and the founder of her own company. It was time for her to step out from behind the scenes.

Marketing is the act of being seen and heard. That means giving our voices, ideas, and stories—complete with wounds and scars—the breathing room they need to exist and take up space. When we don't, it's usually because we are being overly protective of ourselves, but staying behind the scenes and blending into the background sends the wrong message. It says that we don't matter, that other people are more important or more worthy of attention.

How often do you watch fellow entrepreneurs promote their work on social media while you doubt that anyone wants to hear about the new blog you just published?

It takes an extraordinary amount of courage to put yourself out there and risk criticism, disagreement, and worst of all, judgment. But for marginalized communities that traditionally have not had mainstream representation, it's even more imperative for you to show up and be seen.

One woman in my mentoring group told me she was worried about people not buying from her because of the color of her skin. In 2022, we are still worried about being discriminated against and with

---

*   *Name changed for anonymity*

valid reason! Her words speak to all the times she and people of color everywhere have been discriminated against solely based on how we look. Racism is all around us, but we can't give up. The work for us now is undoing years of mental programming that would rather have us hide than show up freely and unapologetically as ourselves. As minority communities and underrepresented groups, we need to see ourselves in places where we're not often represented. It communicates the message that we DO matter and that we belong. When we see people who look like us and understand our stories, it sparks something within us, and we see broader possibilities.

In the age of social media, attention, visibility, and exposure are some of the most important factors for business success. If we continue to stay behind the scenes, we are going to have a tougher time standing out and making the impact we need to make.

Marketing through Storytelling

At the heart of marketing is storytelling; using your voice to share your story and create room for all who see themselves in it. People are moved by stories that speak to the heart of their experiences. Dig deep. Tell the story about what brought you where you are. What were your defining moments? Your biggest life lessons? What inspired you to start your business? And most of all, *why* do you do what you do? Your overall purpose connects to what you do, so always start with your story.

As an entrepreneur, you must know how to pitch herself, whether to a potential investor, a potential client, or the woman you struck up a conversation with standing in line at the grocery store. Use every interaction as an opportunity to tell people who you are and what you do—and do it in sixty seconds flat. The pitch must speak to your *why* and the impact your work has, not just what you do.

I am on a mission to help Black women in business go from surviving to thriving in their career. As an entrepreneur and professional status quo breaker, I interrupt toxic generational patterns that keep us stuck so we can live well at work and beyond. This is the impact I make through my work every day. When I introduce someone to my work, my pitch sounds something like this:

> I'm Ariane and I'm a career equity consultant, author, and speaker. My mission is to build a better future of work for Black women. With over a decade dedicated to coaching Black women to excel in their careers, my approach is anything but conventional. My eye for data allows me to unearth hidden patterns and opportunities in the workplace, transforming them into actionable strategies. I understand the hustle and the resilience it takes to build dreams from the ground up. My lived experience ties it all together, providing a deeply personal touch to my work, ensuring every strategy is not just effective but empathetic. Together, we'll not just navigate the career landscape; we'll redefine it, making it a place where Black women don't just belong but thrive and lead.

Now it's your turn. Take out a sheet of paper and answer the following:

We are a (*what you do*) **and we help** (*ideal client*) **with** (*solution you offer*) **so that they can** (*results you provide*).

We believe that (*mission/vision*) **in order to** (*desired impact you want to achieve*).

Avoid going into the *how* of what you do or the process by which you get your results. People are less interested in that part than whether you can solve their problem.

Know Your Audience

The next key to being an effective marketer is to know your audience. Who are they? Who does your work serve? These are your ideal clients. All too often, new business owners skip over this step of really getting to know their target market. Or even worse, they try to appeal to everyone and cast a wide net to attract more people. This sounds like a logical approach, but when you are trying to speak to everyone, you end up speaking to no one. People respond differently when they know you're speaking directly to them as opposed to a mass audience. When they feel *seen* by you, it creates a more powerful connection.

Knowing your audience means going beyond demographic information. What keeps them up at night? What are their lifestyle habits? What do they value in life? At work? What is their unique situation, the one that prompts them to seek your services? Know your ideal customer better than they know themselves. This is how you are better able to serve them and build products that actually make their lives better. Knowing specifically who you are marketing to takes time, but it is so worth the effort.

Your Message

All great marketing must drive home a message that will connect with consumers. Your message is your means of communicating with your target audience. It's how you talk about your business and what you do. To be on brand, all of your social media and website copy, blog posts, videos, or any other marketing tools used in your business should carry consistent messaging.

In order to be effective, your message must speak to the heart, not just the mind. People want to feel something when you speak to them. Your message should be about the people you serve, their needs, their hopes, their dreams. Be succinct and focused with your message. Present one simple idea that is easy to grasp. When you're all over the place, people start to check out mentally. Your message must bridge the gap between your customers problem and your solution. Give them clear steps of where they are and where they want to be. Oh and lastly: be memorable. Brands try all sorts of theatrics to get you to remember them but being memorable doesn't always have to be loud and in your face. Sometimes the best brands that rise to the top are the ones that are intentionally understated.

How do you want people to feel after hearing your message? Do you want your message to: inspire, motivate, educate, empower, or maybe all of the above? What action do you want people to take?

Consider this example of Patrice Washington's podcast, *Redefining Wealth*. She describes her podcast this way: "Redefining Wealth is NOT your typical personal finance show. We're not here to talk about cutting coupons or budgeting. I'm here to help you live your life's purpose, find fulfillment, and chase purpose—not money."[29]

Or this example from Dr. Uché Blackstock's healthcare consultancy, Advancing Health Equity. Her website states: "AHE can help healthcare organizations to understand the root causes of current-day racialized health inequities and provide strategies to help close the gaps."[30]

In each of these examples, the message is beautifully articulated and speaks directly to the reader. In the first example, the conversational tone uses relatable examples that reflect the reader. The second example says exactly who their work is for and names the results clients can expect in a tone branded toward academic or private entities.

Which of the above messaging resonates with you? It's likely one that can help you develop your own.

Choose Your Stage (Marketing Channel)

I love that marketing takes on so many different forms. Generally, marketing entails anything that exposes your business in a way that compels customers to take action. You can market online, in person, or even at the grassroots level with simple tasks like passing out flyers. Your business might already have a Facebook or Instagram account, but have you considered blogging, networking, starting a newsletter, creating a podcast, or getting interviewed by one? Starting a YouTube video series or leading a workshop in your local community? Putting on events or speaking at a conference?

---

29   Patrice Washington, "It's Time to Prosper," November 17, 2022, in *Redefining Wealth* podcast, Episode 280, MP3 audio, 47:43, https://patricewashington.com/listen/.

30   Dr. Uché Blackstock, "Advancing Healthcare Equity," https://advancinghealthequity.com/.

With so many different ways to create business exposure, it's easy to feel overwhelmed. Should you be on Twitter, TikTok, AND write a blog?! I can hear you saying, "I don't have time for all that, Ariane!" Trust me, I get it. You may think you need to be doing all the things to market your business, but that's simply not true!

In the early days of my business, I wrote a blog that I published once every week and *maaaaybe* had a business Facebook page where I would post from time to time. For the first few years of building my business, I picked one platform that appealed to me—my blog—and worked the hell out of it instead of spreading myself too thin across multiple platforms. I learned how to blog and built an audience through writing.

Each published blog post became a direct marketing channel that created awareness of my work and led readers to my website. In the early days, I wrote about my ideas, things that inspired me and my personal journey of building my own business for the first time. I wrote about everything I went through as a new entrepreneur, even the tough and challenging stuff. I had to be real as I told my story. In a lot of ways, blogging was an outlet and my way of connecting with readers by sharing my intimate thoughts. Truth and honesty about my journey created a trust-building hook. I enjoyed writing, and I was good at it, so it naturally became my medium of choice for business exposure. If writing is not your thang, explore other ways to get your voice out there. Speaking from the heart might come more naturally to you than writing, so public speaking gigs would probably make more sense for you.

No matter what form your marketing takes, it's about tapping into what you naturally do best and leveraging that skill. In the early stages of your business, resist the urge to do everything. Just pick a lane and stick to it. Get good at it. Focus on building traction in that lane. Eventually, you can branch out and grow into other platforms. This will simplify your life—trust me.

Think of marketing as simply choosing the stage you want to step into to get the message out about your business. What stage do you choose? Here are a few of the more common ones:

- Speaking
- Publishing articles on media platforms
- Blogging
- Brand partnerships
- Podcasting
- Videos (YouTube, Facebook/IG Live)
- Social Media (Instagram, Facebook, Twitter)
- Newsletters

Keep it simple and choose between two to three platforms to focus on for your marketing. Avoid trying to be in all the places; you'll only wear yourself thin. Choose the ones that you are already on and focus there.

Make it Measurable

Sweet, sweet data. Marketing can be fun and creative but don't forget to track your data. Data will help you stay grounded in your business by illustrating how well your marketing strategies are performing. How are you tracking your marketing results? You don't want to put loads of effort into marketing without knowing if it's actually working.

Take a moment to identify the data points you want to measure. For example, you can track the growth of your social media fans or email subscribers over time, the open and click rate of your newsletters, the traffic to your website, the number of consultations booked month over month, and the number of product buys. You can look at metrics like engagement; people who bookmarked your posts, forwarded it, or commented on it. Track what posts garner the most comments, for example. These are the ones you want to pay attention to and make more content about since they strongly resonate with your audience. There are many tools available to help you track data for your business. By tracking your progress, you can make any necessary changes as you go along.

The road to mastering the marketing game requires commitment and consistency. Create, test, improve, repeat. Have compassion with yourself and don't be afraid to experiment with different forms of marketing. This is how you become better over time. Marketing is a mindset. There are some very practical ways to boost your visibility, and taking these steps will help teach you how to powerfully take up space and share who you are without sacrificing your integrity.

Purpose to Practice

Now that your marketing juices are flowing, and you're ready to get out there, here's where to start:

1. **Determine your business marketing goals.** The choice is as broad as your imagination and might include more followers, paid clients, exposure for your product or service, paid sponsorships from high profile brands or something else altogether. Consider this goal list from a client of mine who owns and operates a yoga studio:

   a. Become the go-to source for healing through healthy juice remedies and body strengthening classes

   b. Increase class attendance by 20 percent

   c. Grow online presence of studio by adding 1,000 followers

2. **Start where you feel the most comfortable.** If you're a good writer, you may want to start blogging or writing thought leadership pieces. If you're good in front of the camera, you may want to explore doing more video content of yourself teaching a series or speaking on a topic that you know is a common problem for your target audience.

3. **Pick ONE channel to focus on.** Remember, in the beginning there's no need for you to be everywhere at once. Ideally, it's a platform where you already spend most of your time. Focus there first, master it, then add from there.

4. **Balance your content type.** I recommend to my clients that 80

percent of their posts/content must add value in some way and 20 percent can be promotional. That means, at least 80 percent of your post should be valuable content that teaches, gives, inspires, or otherwise empowers people to easily do something on their own.

Remember, be fearless, stay consistent, and start small. You got this.

Chapter 7

MENTORSHIP AND BUILDING
UP YOUR ARMY OF ANGELS

AFTER HIGH SCHOOL, I'D HAD enough of being one of very few Black people in the classroom. I wanted a different experience. One where I could bring my homecooked curry goat leftovers to school for lunch, and no one would gawk at my food and ask, "What is that?" An experience where I could rock box braids and no one would say, "Oh, my God, your hair grew so long!" I distinctly remember wanting to surround myself with people who looked like me and whose experiences I could relate to. I wanted to see more teachers of color in the classrooms and to finally know more of my history. I yearned for real life examples to show me that it was possible for Black folks to succeed—and not just on television. It was decided. I would enroll at an HBCU.

When I attended Lincoln University the first degree-granting HBCU, it was the first time in my young adult life, I saw Black and brown teachers—albeit mostly men. They were PhDs and award-winning professors who played pivotal roles in shaping the hearts and minds of future leaders. The president of my university was a Black man, and the Dean was a tall, Black woman, with brown hair and a mighty presence. Her name was Dr. Judith Thomas, and I was completely enthralled by her.

Dr. Thomas had a commanding presence wherever she went. All she had to do was walk into a room and all eyes would be on her with adoration, attention, and respect. She was passionate about her students and took her job very seriously. She was sometimes especially hard on us as she pushed and challenged us to higher aspirations through education. She never let us forget whom we were or where we came from, and she made it clear that we had a duty to continue paving the way and lifting each other up. Dr. Thomas would always remind us, "As educated Black leaders, you must pass the baton."

Knowing how hard my ancestors fought for my right to exist, take up space, and claim my birthright as a Black woman in this country, this message means more to me now than it did back then. We have an incredible opportunity to no longer be the "only" one occupying the spaces we are in. With that opportunity comes the responsibility to ensure those coming up behind us have an easier path, so we must share knowledge and resources openly to create truly collaborative spaces. In many ways, Dr. Thomas was my first mentor, a role model of a highly respected Black woman established in her career and leadership. I wanted to be just like her.

However, while college exposed me to the Black experience I had craved, it wasn't reflective of the real world. By the time I got well into my corporate career, most times I was one of few women of color present. Again.

Sometimes the workplace can expose us to mentors, but when diversity is lacking, it can be hard to attain the type of mentorship we most need. I was accustomed to seeing mostly white men and women in senior leadership positions. There definitely weren't many examples of high-powered, Black women holding leadership positions available to me back then. And because I didn't see them, I was at a loss for how to create that kind of success in my own career.

Much of what I learned about how to get ahead and survive at work was by playing the assimilation game. From the grad school I attended, how I dressed, and how I wore my hair to where I spent after-work happy hours and even how much or how little I spoke up in meetings, I was influenced by the people around me. It's hard to follow the guidance of a mentor who doesn't have to assimilate to get ahead.

Even as I struck out on my own, access to other Black women entrepreneurs were few and far between. I had supportive connections from a few folks and had eventually hired a business coach, but for the first few years of my business, I had to mostly just figure it out. I followed prescriptive career advice from self-help and career leadership books written by people who did not look like me nor shared my experience—books like *Nice Girls Don't Get the Corner Office* by Lois Frankel (2004) and of course, Sheryl Sandberg's *Lean In* (2013). I followed advice from top white voices in the game, like Marie Forleo, Gabrielle Bernstein, Danielle LaPorte—all successful entrepreneurs whose success I wanted to emulate. I loaded up on their books, took workshops, and bought expensive trainings every chance I could. I even traveled across the country to attend a conference in California led by some guy named Ted who claimed charismatically that he could teach you how to have a six-figure business. No shade to Ted, but in retrospect, there wasn't anything really that special about him; he just had a lot of mediocre white man energy. But at the time, I ate it up. You name it, I did it. As an early-stage entrepreneur, I was hungry, and I would have done whatever it took to learn from "the best," so I could be successful like them.

I spent a lot of time with other successful entrepreneurs to see what I could learn from them. I bought them lunch to "pick their brains" about business advice. I attended the same networking circles as they did. I worked closely with them to learn as much as I could. In a sense, they were my unofficial mentors, and I did learn a lot from the people whose work I respected. But in all honesty, these were people who did not know the first thing about being a Black woman in business because that was not their experience. It wasn't until I became exposed to the work of Carla Harris, Latham Thomas, Cyndie Spiegel, Minda Harts, and so many other fabulous Black women that I began to get a taste of how much melanin was actually in the entrepreneurial ecosystem.

Deep sigh of relief.

Our Earliest Mentors

When you're not exposed to people who look like you or do what you aspire to do, it becomes incredibly difficult to see beyond your own limited perspective. Visibility matters.

Seeing other Black women entrepreneurs who mirrored my image showed me what was glaringly missing and still hard to find—Black women leaders. This is not to say they do not exist. Quite the contrary. They are in our households, our churches, in the office, or running for office. They are also running six, seven, and multi-figure businesses. Hello, Folorunsho Alakija! (Google her.)

These are the role models we need to see every day to know what is possible, to illustrate the wide range of successful entrepreneurship. We must see greatness to inspire and stretch our own levels of leadership.

You don't need billions of dollars in the bank to lead, nor do you need a fancy title. Stepping up to lead comes from a deep desire to pave the way and create opportunities for those around you. As I mentioned earlier, my first examples of women leaders and mentors were the women in my family—my mother, my aunts, and my grandmother. In order to know where you're going, you must first understand who you are and where you came from. So much of who we are as women relates to the qualities and traits we inherit from our earliest role models. What did we learn from them? How do we reflect some of the same actions, behaviors, and beliefs? And how do we become our own version of great women leaders so that we can help shape the next generation?

In a word, the women of my family were *strong*. They emigrated from their home country of Jamaica to the US in search of better opportunities for their family. All they knew how to be was strong and resilient, and to persevere; traits that I am positive were passed down to them from their mamas, grandmamas, and great-grandmamas. Women of my mother's and grandmother's generations were counted on to be many things; they were the glue that held everything together.

Growing up, I watched the women in my family raise us kids, run a household, work extremely hard, overcome difficult challenges, and sacrifice, over and over again. They were matriarchs, nurturers, lovers, caregivers, confidants, healers, and incredible pillars of wisdom who protected their loved ones and held it all together, day after day.

My grandmother was the matriarch of my family and a dreamer in her own way. While spending most of her life in Jamaica, she held onto her dream of coming to the US to build a life for herself and her family. At the time, she had a friend in Canada who told her to leave Jamaica, send for her kids, and never go back. Grandma left for Canada, stayed with her friend on a travel visa, took a bus across state lines, and arrived in New York in 1972. She rode that bus from Canada to Boston to New York while terrified that she would get busted and sent back to Jamaica. Her choice to come to the US without her kids was incredibly difficult. She took a major risk, not knowing if everything would work out the way she imagined. If she failed, it would not only affect her but her children as well. She did it anyway, knowing that there was a larger goal at stake.

Once settled in New York, Grandma immediately began working as domestic help and nanny for a white family. She spent every day cleaning, cooking, scrubbing floors until her hands were raw, and looking after young children. She scraped up every dollar she could earn until she had enough money for her children in Jamaica—including my mom—to join her in the US. Had she not taken this risk, I would not be here. In the US, she was not handed an opportunity; she created one. With determination and perseverance, she carved a new path and led her family to a place where they would thrive. Despite her fear, my grandmother stepped up to lead because she had to. It wasn't a choice.

This kind of leadership is prevalent in many households, especially within immigrant families. The women we know as mothers, grandmothers, sisters, aunts, wives, girlfriends, students, best friends, managers, CEOs, and entrepreneurs who lead every single day, contribute so much to help change the world around us. They do not take a day off. They do not complain. They simply rise with faith, courage, and vulnerability to pave the way for the rest of us.

We come from a long ancestral lineage of great women leaders. It's in our DNA. The sheroes we saw as little Black and Brown girls helped mold us to become the women we are today. We create a ripple effect by deciding who we want to be as leaders and the impact we leave on others.

The power we have as women is manifold. Our words, actions, and belief in ourselves have the power to effect real change. It begins in our homes with our families and extends to our communities, the workplace, our businesses, and finally the world. Rising up into leadership has never been more imperative; we must show each other the way through sisterhood, truth, and unshakeable courage.

Mentoring and Being Mentored

After the sixth year of my business, I hit a wall. I'd spent a lot of money working with several coaches throughout the years, many of whom happened to be white, and I needed a new approach. While I received great support from these coaches, the truth was I did not feel seen by them. A lot of times, I left my sessions feeling alone. I knew I needed to change who I looked to for support. It was then I decided I wanted a Black woman mentor. I wanted to see myself in someone older, wiser, smarter and who would understand the unique challenges that I had as a Black woman in business. It was important to me to build relationships with other women of color in business who were doing the things I wanted to do. As we continue to progress by leaps and bounds as the fastest growing group of entrepreneurs, mentorship will be key to maintaining our growth trajectory.

It's said that when the student is ready, the teacher will appear. Well, the Universe must have heard my prayers because only a few months later, I met the person who ultimately became my mentor. One afternoon in early November, I was invited to attend an Academi of Life conference, "The Things That Really Matter" featuring several motivational speakers. Yes, sign me up!

I got dressed and traveled from my Brooklyn apartment on a cold, wintry day all the way to the Upper West Side of Manhattan. I made my way towards the venue, The Academi of Life. Inside the venue, I walked along the green-painted walls toward the auditorium. I grabbed a seat in the audience toward the front and listened intently to each speaker on stage. Each spoke for ten minutes on all kinds of topics from self-mastery and resilience to mental well-being. I sat in complete adoration as the speakers shared their stories and intimate bits of their lives.

The last person to take the stage was a beautiful, dark-skinned woman with a Spanish accent and a glowing smile. She spoke about self-mastery, mindfulness, and adopting more holistic approaches to business. I had been to a lot of self-improvement talks before, but rarely did I see anyone share their story of overcoming challenges in her career so vulnerably, especially as a Black woman in business. I felt like she was speaking to me personally.

"One day my life changed in a major way," she said, and the audience fell silent. "I was let go from my comfortable job and suddenly the arguments that I kept telling myself were no longer valid. The prestige, the status, what other people thought. None of it mattered anymore."

I hung onto her every word. This woman spoke from her heart and never wavered. I knew right away that I wanted to work with her—Bisila Bokoko—an international entrepreneur, philanthropist, global speaker, and champion for living your best life. The woman even has her own wine company! I mean yes, come through, Black Girl Magic!

After Bisila's talk that night, I couldn't wait to meet her. I walked up and introduced myself and shared how much I enjoyed her talk. We exchanged business cards and decided to keep in touch. After a few emails back and forth, and following Bisila's extraordinary work online, I wanted to learn more. I had already made up my mind that she would be my mentor. But how? I had no idea if she would want to work with me or if she even did that kind of thing, but I went out on a limb and made a bold ask.

I invited Bisila to lunch one afternoon at Le Pain Quotidien, a cute little restaurant near Madison Square Park in New York City.

"Two please," I said to the hostess when I arrived at the restaurant a bit early for my meeting with Bisila. The hostess showed me to a table for two on the second floor with sprawling windows overlooking Broadway and the park nearby.

I was a bit nervous as I awaited Bisila's arrival. I mentally rehearsed my talking points, anxious to impress her and show her that I was worth her time.

After several minutes, Bisila arrived. She greeted me with a big smile and a hug as though we had known each other for years. We exchanged small talk for a few minutes, ordered salads from the menu, and then settled into our conversation. I was so eager to jump in and share more with her about why I wanted to meet with her.

"So tell me about you, Ariane. What is it that you do?" Her Spanish accent gave a lyrical rhythm to her words;.

I couldn't wait to get to know her better. "I am a business owner," I began. "I'm on a mission to empower as many Black women in their careers as I can. I started my own career consultancy five years ago, and I am ready to grow as an entrepreneur." I'm pretty sure my voice cracked a bit as I tried to get my story out, but I was assured by Bisila's expression that she was listening intently.

At first, she sat quietly and just listened as I spoke. Inside, I was freaking out. The woman in front of me was someone whose work I widely respected and who took time out of her busy schedule to meet with me. I had done a lot of homework on Bisila, so I wanted to impress her with my thorough research. Then she would know just how serious I was about working with her.

As I spoke, I wondered what she thought of me and my work. She was so used to speaking with high-powered business people and global companies, I wondered why she would even give me the time of day. But I must have said something right—or maybe she could see herself in me through the passion in my voice—because when I paused, she immediately responded.

"Ariane," she said, "it sounds like you're doing wonderful work, but stepping into this level of leadership is no easy task. I want you to ask yourself if you *really* want this, because to get to where you want to be, you must be ready to work." Her soft, gentle demeanor turned fierce and no nonsense as she continued. "I only take on a small number of mentees a year, and to work with me, you have to stay committed and not waste my time."

Whoa! Bisila was all about her business and did not want her time to be wasted. The self-mastery and how she asserted her boundaries felt intimidating, but that kind of leadership made me want to work with her even more. These were exactly the type of skills I wanted to learn for myself. I would be required to work harder than I'd ever worked before, to step out of my comfort zone, to show up at every mentoring session with her prepared and ready to learn, and stay committed to doing the work. I agreed with every fiber of my being. Yet deep down, I feared failure. I worried that I didn't have what it took to step into the level of leadership that I so desperately wanted. At the same time, I was afraid of disappointing myself and my mentor.

Many of us struggle with the fear of failing ourselves and failing others. Still, that day, I decided to bet on myself. Bisila and I entered into a contract to make it official, and I paid her to mentor me. Yes, this was no ordinary mentor-mentee arrangement. We signed a contract, and I paid for the privilege of working with Bisila because I highly valued the benefit that she would bring. And so did she because working with her was *not* cheap. I was happy to pay for the experience and a structured mentor relationship.

We agreed to meet weekly, each time focusing on a specific aspect of my growth as a leader and the development of my business. Sometimes we think of working with mentors in one-off conversations here and there throughout our career. That wasn't enough for me. Building new habits and learning techniques to change the trajectory of your life and career won't happen if you do it once and hope for the best. I wanted the benefit of ongoing, consistent conversations with my mentor, gleaning concrete advice to meet goals over a specified period of time. I wanted the structure and the accountability of someone I admired and respected.

I didn't take mentoring with Bisila lightly. I was ready to do the work.

Being mentored shaped me to play a bigger game in life, work, and personal leadership. In the beginning, however, I really didn't know what I was in for. I thought we would immediately jump into business mechanics, and I came prepared with a list of goals I anxiously wanted to accomplish. They were specific goals: double my income, be featured in top business journals, land more high-profile speaking engagements, and on and on.

"We'll get there eventually," Bisila said, "but first things first." Instead of diving headfirst into the how-tos, she sent me within. I had to work on my mindset. Bisila called it "cleaning out the house."

"Cleaning out the house" meant working on all the doubts and old stories that had long been sabotaging my success. And we had to do this BEFORE we started any work on my business.

I wanted no part of it.

Talk about being resistant! I wanted to skip over this part because a) I had done enough work on myself already, or so I thought; and b) deep emotional work was something I regularly did for my clients. Doing it for myself was a whole other thing. All the more reason why there was so much more work I needed to do! Things like undoing the negative money beliefs I had learned as a child and even forgiving people in my life whom I still blamed. I *had* to clean my house.

I started waking up earlier to begin my day with new, inspiring morning routines. I started cooking meals at home for myself rather than ordering takeout constantly. Spending quality time in the kitchen putting together delicious meals for myself reminded me of what it's like to put my health first and choose meals that would nourish my body instead of just satisfy my hunger. I even began doing things unrelated to my business, just for fun. All of this taught me how to treat and love myself well. To my surprise, many of these practices were very hard for me to do. I had to unlearn how to stop reaching for success and just *become* success for myself first and foremost.

Through the experience of being mentored, I learned that becoming a successful entrepreneur was about more than creating a six figure income; it was about discovering how taking care of mind, body, and heart would make me better in business. If you want to be a millionaire, you first have to treat yourself like a million bucks. My mentor had an untraditional way of teaching business success and fulfillment; through her I learned that it must always begin with an internal focus.

I learned to be a student again and actively absorbed the wisdom and leadership of someone who had done everything I aspired to do. I learned how to see myself as a brand with a purpose and a businesswoman. I learned how to leverage my talents and experiences in a way that opened doors for me. For one assignment, Bisila had me raise my prices to a really uncomfortable amount that I didn't think anyone would pay. But they did! I landed a five-figure contract with a client in just one month. I was floored. Bisila taught me how to structure my fees by focusing on the value I provided to my clients. It sounds so simple, but it was incredibly difficult when I had tried to do it on my own.

In one of our sessions, Bisila put me on the spot and asked, "Why should people hire you?" It wasn't a rhetorical question, she literally had me explain why people should hire me. This exercise helped me to clearly state my value, what I offered that was different, and how to confidently communicate those points to my clients. It became so much clearer how to position myself to attract clients. Shortly after that, I started booking larger contracts effortlessly.

My network expanded as a result of partnering with my mentor; she opened up her rolodex of high-profile business leaders and basically went on a spree introducing me to everyone on her VIP list. I was invited into her inner circle of other women leaders who, after forging connections with them, also opened doors for me. Invitations to speak on larger stages started to appear. I was even invited to speak at an annual women's conference in Africa. Africa! Yes, the motherland!

The time, money, and emotional investment I had put into working with a mentor paid off threefold. The value and confidence I saw in myself doubled and then tripled because of the potential my mentor saw in me. I learned to see it in myself. That, for me, was worth its weight in gold. In a world where women are pitted against each other, it can be so incredibly hard to see ourselves as collaborators and not competitors. Working with my mentor was a true testament to what we can achieve by learning to lift each other up through generosity and a strong desire to see our sisters succeed.

Women of color, particularly Black women, tell me that they prefer to be mentored by women who look like them and occupy roles they aspire to. Yet, some of the most common impediments we face in finding mentors especially as we get into our 30s and 40s include not actively seeking mentorship, the intimidation felt by initiating a mentoring relationship, and sometimes, just not knowing where to look.

Working intentionally with a highly successful Black woman entrepreneur as my mentor was hands down one of the best decisions I could have made to grow my career and business. Bisila taught me by example how to break down stereotypes, to demand a seat at the table, and actually to occupy the room where the most powerful decisions are made. She showed me how to bet on myself when no one else would bother, to know my worth, and how to translate that worth into real dollars in my bank account. You need mentors who will be with you, even during the tough periods. My mentor was with me through the tough moments when I had to pick myself up off the floor from failure and setbacks. It just hits differently for women of color when you have someone *like you* who is consistently in your corner supporting you.

Cultivating a Mentoring Relationship

Mentoring is an ancient practice. It first appeared in Greek mythology around 1200 BCE when Odysseus asked his bestie—who was actually named "Mentor"—to serve as a guide, advisor, and friend to his son Telemachus while he was away at war. A mentoring relationship was officially formed.

The art of mentoring became more modernized in the 1970s to cultivate the growth and development of those seeking to learn from people more experienced in specific areas. It was most often practiced in workplaces to develop corporate executives. Since then, it continues to be a trusted tool in many business communities.

Thanks to technology, mentoring has evolved. We now have access to more people from all over the world who can guide our careers. On social media, we can follow and learn from our favorite leaders and thinkers in any industry. What they do and say oftentimes influences our own work and career. Most times, we look up to people whom we may not know personally, but whose work we respect and influences us. Although this may be a more unofficial mentorship without the traditional one-on-one relationship or titles of mentor-mentee, we are still learning and growing from their guidance.

Structured mentoring relationships, like the one I had with Bisila, are more focused and individualized, but either way, learning from a mentor is priceless.

Finding and Working with A Mentor

So, you are ready to work with a mentor. There are a few ways you might find one. Let's say you work for a company full time. You might start with your company's leadership chain. Find a few people from a different department or with different functions and perspectives than you have, people you respect and would like to learn from.

What if you're an entrepreneur? You may want to be a bit more creative with your approach. First, you'll want to find your community, a place where other entrepreneurs hang out. You can try your local Chamber of Commerce, business networking events, workshops, or conferences. Now that more events are happening virtually through webinars, Slack communities, and other online networks, we have even more opportunities to make connections and access communities across the globe.

Whenever you attend an organized event—online or off—get into the practice of introducing yourself to the speakers. This is a great networking tactic; even if it doesn't turn into a mentoring relationship, it will at the very least expand your connections. Once you've introduced yourself, follow up via email or LinkedIn with a personalized note. Set reminders to follow up with your new connections occasionally so you can continue to build the relationship over time. This also helps you stay on the radar of those you are serious about connecting with.

Building Mentor Relationships

When you're beginning to get to know a potential mentor, make sure it's the right match before you establish an official mentor-mentee relationship. The only way to know it's right is to take your time in building the relationship and consider what you want to get out of it. What are your goals? What is important for you to have in a mentor? Is it their résumé or number of followers? Do they value the same things as you do? Are they knowledgeable in their industry? Have they accomplished the things you most desire to do? Does their personality align with yours?

Yeah. Finding a good mentor is much like dating to find "the one."

One note of caution: Most people like the idea of being a mentor but not everyone can or should be one. At a minimum, you want to make sure the person mentoring you has certain qualities. Being an active listener for one. Being empathetic, a good thought partner, having enthusiasm for sharing and teaching their expertise to others. They should be respectful and nonjudgmental but not afraid to be honest, even if the truth hurts. Somebody's gotta tell you when your business idea sucks! But do it with love, of course.

Do some light stalking. By that, I mean conduct some research on the person you are interested in mentoring with. Learn about their background and determine how it fits in with your goals. Be ready with facts upon facts about the person's career so you're clear on what they've done and how it fits in with your goals. Not only is this impressive, but it helps them to see you are serious, you have done your homework, and that you are not about to waste their time or yours.

So, you're ready to make your move. Before asking someone to be your mentor, make sure you have targeted goals so that your potential mentor can evaluate their ability to help you. Goals also help shape the format and structure for working together.

When you're ready to ask your potential mentor to go steady with you—told ya, it's a lot like dating!—I always recommend that you talk to them "live." You can begin with an email inviting them to lunch or coffee. If meeting in person is not possible, speak by phone or video conference.

I helped a good friend of mine connect with a mentor, a high-profile woman whose long list of impressive accomplishments was a bit intimidating. It made her nervous. My friend worried that this woman would be way too busy to mentor her, or that she was too "small potatoes" for the woman to even give her the time of day. All very legitimate concerns. But in the famous words of my mother, "If you don't ask, you don't get."

No truer words have been spoken. I hear those words in my head every single time I want something but I'm too afraid to ask. We can't let our doubts and assumptions about things hold us back from asking. There is so much gold on the other side of an ask, especially when it's a scary-to-make ask. The scarier the ask, the bigger the pot of gold. At the very worst, the person you're asking can say *no*, in which case you would pick your face up off the floor, dust it off, and keep going.

Sometimes a *no* just means *not now*, in which case the timing may not be right. It may sting a little hearing *no*, but at least you can be proud to know that you tried. But when you don't ask at all, you get nothing PLUS the regret of never knowing. Don't be that person; always make the ask.

PS: My friend did ask her very high-profile mentor crush to be her mentor—and she said yes!

Put Away the Strong, Independent Black Woman Narrative

I need to address another common challenge I see facing Black women: the strong, independent woman narrative. This is a common challenge for women in general, but I think we have internalized to our detriment the particular stigma of being a strong *Black* woman.

As Black women, we come from a long ancestral line of hardworking women with a fierce commitment to independence that, in many ways, came because they had no choice. Generations of women in my family faced incredible challenges but persevered on their own. I am so proud to come from this line of women who were strong in mind, body, and spirit no matter what adversity they encountered. I've watched the women in my family just *handle* shit. They didn't think about it—they just jumped in and took whatever action was necessary. They worked hard and never complained. They took on a lot because most times, no one else was going to. There wasn't anyone waiting in the wings to say, "It's okay, you can rest." Historically, Black women were thought to be able to tolerate higher thresholds of pain. Not just physical pain but emotional and mental pain. This expectation of brute strength and high threshold for emotional pain has programmed us to suffer in silence to feel as though we can't ask for help or that we don't deserve it. Asking for help is very hard to do when the people around you think that you don't need it or believe that you're tough, you can handle it.

As someone who runs her own business while living and working in New York City, I have, on more than one occasion, lauded myself as fiercely independent. Helping other people was what I did for a living, but when it came to myself, it was hard for me to receive help. Looking back, nothing but my ego prevented me from asking for help. I am proud of my independence and how it has served me, but I recognize just how much my resistance to asking for help actually held me back. The default mode for juggling the demands of life and work is to push through and figure it out on our own. Even when we are working hard to build our dreams and aspiring to the next level, we often hold on to this "It's me against the world" complex.

Why do we do this? Why do we feel we have to fight fires alone? Part of this thinking comes from our actual lived experiences; we were strong because we had to be. But just because we can handle the fire on our own doesn't mean we have to. It's time society stops seeing us as superhumans but as humans vulnerable to mental and emotional exhaustion just like anyone else. And it's time we stop pushing beyond our own capacity to live up to this damaging narrative. It's time to ask those around us for help.

While there is no limit to the magnitude and power of what we can achieve and create in the world, we don't have to do it alone. I have personally witnessed the magic that happens when we form together as a collective sisterhood and get shit done.

The most priceless result? The sheer calm and relief we feel when an army of angels descends, ready to support us.

Life on its own is tough enough. Call on your community. You don't have to do it alone.

Networking and Building Your Army of Angels

Raise your hand if you enjoy networking. You know, going to stuffy business events, handing out your business card. When we hear the word "networking," it reeks of gross interactions with people we don't know to see if we can get something out of it, whether it be new business, new clients, or some other new opportunity. And let's be real, we've all been on the receiving side of that bad energy when someone approaches with that car salesy vibe or tries to pitch a deal. When we think about networking for the sake of our business or generating new clients, it can often feel inauthentic.

I mentioned in previous chapters that I'm an introvert and the idea of socializing in large groups like networking events isn't my idea of a fun time. But what's helped me to embrace networking and ease my anxiety around it is viewing networking as a way to meet and connect with interesting people without any expectations. I genuinely enjoy meeting other entrepreneurs and learning about what people are working on, so I use this curiosity to connect with people authentically.

When you go in with the intention to meet and connect with new people and build new relationships, regardless of whether that relationship leads to a sale, it takes the pressure off. There's no need to impress or perform. Networking, then, shifts from how you can further your own agenda to an experience of you connecting meaningfully with other people and being of service to them.

The same rules that apply to finding a mentor—or "the one"—apply to networking. Know what you're looking for and assess the best places to find it. Go to conferences, sign up for workshops, attend industry events, or get active on LinkedIn. Like looking for any type of partnership, there's no one way to do it. Surround yourself with a tribe of other entrepreneurs who get what you're doing. Many of your days—especially in the early years of building your business—can be isolating and lonely. In the beginning, when you don't have a lot of clients or a team, it's hard to stay motivated and build momentum in your business. Working in isolation can often bring up anxiety, worry, overthinking, overanalyzing, and perfectionism.

To break out of this pattern, I went to coffee shops and even hotel lounges with good Wi-Fi to set up my laptop and work. Being out in the world and being around other freelancers and nontraditional workers gave me the fuel and interaction I needed to feel like I was part of a collective energy. I also used coworking spaces to build my community and be among a network of colleagues whom I could exchange ideas with and refer work to. Even if I didn't know them personally, there was this unspoken language of, *We're all in this together.*

The Power of Many

I first heard the idea of mastermind groups from Napoleon Hill, author of the classic personal development book, *Think and Grow Rich.* He defines the concept of masterminds as the "coordination of knowledge and effort, in a sprit of harmony, between two or more people, for the attainment of a definite purpose."[31] Through group interactions, we can solve problems and receive insight by working together collectively. I

---

31   Napoleon Hill, *Think and Grow Rich*, The Ralston Society (Meriden: 2017 edition), 250-251.

joined a mastermind group where, every two weeks, a group of other entrepreneurs and I met to discuss our business goals and work through challenges together. For two years, we met and never missed a session. What I loved about this was having a group that supported me and challenged me to step up my own game and go farther in my business. Some of these same folks ended up becoming some of my best friends to this day.

Entrepreneurship can be a lonely road, so having a community of like-minded people is key. Surround yourself with people you can be honest with, who will give you open feedback and hold you accountable.

Undoing Networking Nerves

If you Google *networking for entrepreneurs*, you'll get thousands of results about how and where to network. There's no limit to the resources helping you be a better networker. But what about how to navigate networking when it's something we shy away from? I once had a conversation with a senior manager working full time at a prestigious financial services company. She had been with the same company for twenty-plus years and had worked her way up the ladder. She was accomplished at her firm. Everyone liked her; she had even earned awards throughout her time there. When I asked how she did it and what her secret was to being successful at her company, it was not the answer I expected.

She said, "Ariane, I just do good work and stick to myself."

She loathed the idea of politics and networking her way up the corporate ladder. And while her résumé was impressive, I wondered how differently her path would have unfolded if she had been more open to the idea of building professional connections and had intentionally networked throughout her career. Would she have gotten to a more senior level position faster than the twenty-plus years it took if she's had the right people in her corner? Could she have made more money over the years? Would she still be at that company, or would she have secured an even better opportunity elsewhere? I share this example because I know oftentimes, we can tend to keep our heads down and wait for "our turn."

The idea of networking may feel like a transactional, inauthentic way to get what we want, so we'd rather stick it out on our own. I'm with you! I hate that kind of networking too. When someone is only trying to "sell" us on something, we can spot the fakeness from a mile away.

Let's challenge the narrative that networking is an icky, slimy thing that we *have* to do as people in business.

Marketing expert and former Netflix CMO, Bozoma Saint John, often says the principle behind networking is not so much about exchanging contact information and getting the biggest Rolodex, but about creating real relationships. I want to emphasize that last part: *creating real relationships.* The kinds of quality relationships that lead to genuine connection, trust, and reliability. Real relationships develop when you focus on bringing value to the person and your relationship. That means taking the time to get to know someone, finding out what they value and what is important to them, understanding the challenges that get in the way, and what a solution looks like to them. Lead with curiosity when engaging in networking conversations, ask questions, and actively listen. When building a relationship in the beginning, it's about asking more questions instead of doing all the talking. Share new ideas and perspectives as it relates to your industry or the problem that your business solves. Share free insights, resources, and tools that you think might be helpful to the person you're networking with. Make sure they're genuine and can serve as a solution to their problem.

When it comes to networking nerves, here are the most common blocks and what to do about them.

Nervous about going to a networking event alone? Bring a buddy! But don't stick around each other the whole time either. Challenge yourselves to each meet with two new people before the end of the event. True networking thrives on quality over quantity, so rather than "work the room," set an intention to make two meaningful connections by the time you leave.

Nervous about being in a large group? Networking doesn't always have to mean being in a busy room amidst hundreds of people talking at the same time. (My little introverted heart just sped up at just the thought of it.) Set up one-on-one networking coffee chats or lunch meetings with the professionals you want to meet. That way, you get personalized time without all of the distractions. Bonus: If you're an introvert, you're going to rock at this form of networking. You actually might grow to love it!

Nervous about "wasting someone's time"? If you want to set up a networking one-to-one chat and you're worried about whether it will waste their time, my best advice: ask anyway! Remember my mom's adage, "If you don't ask, you don't get." Let the person tell you if they don't have time to meet with you; don't assume.

Nervous about finding other entrepreneurs or mentors to connect with? Start with local coworking spaces, online communities, or Slack channels. Search Eventbrite or Meetup.com for upcoming events or workshops where you know other entrepreneurs will also be in attendance.

The best way to start when it comes to networking is to jump right on in.

Pro tip: When attending virtual events on Zoom or online conference, hop in to the chat box with a gentle hello and the link to your LinkedIn profile in the chat box, and invite others to connect with you there. It's an instant way to get in front of other attendees and make new connections.

What Do You Do? Is Canceled

And while you're out there networking your little tushes off, one more thing I want you to consider. Can we all agree to cancel the infamous question you get asked all the time at networking events: "So, what do you do?" Ugh! Why is this still our go-to conversation starter? It's so boring and mechanical. It's an outdated form of socializing that puts the value on what we do instead of who we are. It's not the best entry point to building meaningful relationships. There's a better way, I promise.

Instead, we can ask, "What are you up to that you're passionate about?" "What new projects are you working on in the world?" "What are you working on that you're excited about?" Can't you just feel the joy and expansion in these questions? This, my friend, is how you network with purpose. Let's lay, "So what do you do for work?" to rest once and for all and move on to better, more meaningful networking conversation starters.

When you're an entrepreneur continually focused on growing your career, your relationships with other professionals in the field will absolutely determine how far you go. We've all heard the saying, "Your network is your net worth." This could not be truer when it comes to building your dreams. You cannot, I repeat, *cannot* do it without people who can help you build. We must enlist the help and support of others to open doors for us, provide resources we don't have access to, and share wisdom and guidance to help us reach our goals. It's incredibly important to find your people.

I've mentioned this before, but it bears repeating: Building a business can feel lonely and isolating a lot of the time. Sometimes your family and friends won't understand the choices you're making as you go after your dreams and do the things that set your heart on fire. When you try to make positive changes in your life, your crew—the one that knows the old you—might not understand the person you're trying to become. Your change makes them feel uncomfortable. It may even make them feel resentful because it leaves them with few excuses for staying put. You might find that people you thought were your friends will abandon you or make you feel guilty for choosing your dreams over them.

That's okay, and it is to be expected as you grow into your power.

Many people in your life will be there for a reason, season, or a lifetime. You will quickly discover what category your friends fall into as you make changes in your life. Those who are genuinely there to support you will take that journey with you. They'll remain your friends for a lifetime. Those who don't only stick around for a season. For every friendship lost, there is another person—or angel, as I like to call them—who will come into your life and help you carry out the things that you were meant to. Similarly, you will enter another person's life to help them on their journey. That's just how it works out most times.

Take comfort in knowing that when you leap toward your dreams, the Universe will send you the exact people you need to help you fulfill them. I've seen it happen more times than I can count.

Your army of angels will give you the wings you need to fly higher than you ever thought possible. They will catch you when you fall, support you, and be a cheerleader for you. They will also tell you the truth when you need to hear it.

We need to continually focus on helping and supporting one another. Throw away the idea of competition. It only holds us back. The mindset that eats us alive inside thinks *If I help someone get what they want, there will not be enough for me.* True angels don't think that way. They are generous, kind, without ego, and they truly want to see their sisters win.

A perfect example of this occurred when Jamaica's Toni-Ann Singh won the Miss World 2019 crown. The moment Toni-Ann's name was announced as the winner, the runner up, Miss Nigeria exploded in excitement, sincerely happy to see her "competition" take the crown. I can't even retell the story without tearing up. It was, in my opinion one of the most genuine displays of camaraderie and sisterhood the world had ever witnessed. *This* is what it means to truly support your sister, to be angels to one another, and to be happy when you see each other win.

We are all part of an interconnected, interdependent tapestry. When one of us reaches a certain level of success, we must never forget those who are following in our footsteps or those who opened doors for us. We must always look to the left and the right, asking who we can help. The more we raise and build each other up, the more power we will have as an army of sisters.

Purpose to Practice

Check Meetup.com, Eventbrite.com, or LinkedIn to search for professional groups and upcoming events tailored to Black women within your industry

You can also explore online communities or coworking spaces. One of my favorites is a New York City based co-working space, Luminary that offers an expansive network of professional women. A a few other favorites are Babel Loft in Brooklyn, and Ethel's Club an online wellness space for people of color

Put two networking events on your calendar to attend within the next thirty days.

Chapter 8
REST CULTURE

IN AN EPISODE OF *In Living Color*, a television sketch comedy show from the nineties, a recurring skit poked fun at Jamaicans for having multiple jobs. And when I say "multiple," I mean at least ten or more. In a really bad impression of a Jamaican accent, the dad, Papa Hedley, would reprimand his son for only having *one* job.

"One job?!" he exclaims, completely appalled by the audacity of his son to have only one single job. "You lazy lima bean. When I was your age, I was a maintenance man, a carpenter, a cab driver, a cook, a hospital orderly, a security guard, a tour guide, a fish cleaner, and an Amway distributor all in the same day."

That episode always sticks out for a couple of reasons. First, because even though it was satire, it was the closest I'd come to seeing Jamaican families represented on mainstream television. And second, I wondered if it were true. What did it mean for us to work hard, and did that really mean having one, two, and maybe even three jobs in order to keep up and to achieve the life that white families could have with just a one- or two income household?

I am proud of our work ethic. You can't say Black women—and especially Caribbean women—are not hardworking. We don't know what it is to not work. Even to this day, when my mother has time off, best believe she'll will find something to do. The woman has a work ethic that won't quit!

Lazy or Luxury

Rest is a very hard thing for many of us to claim without having feelings of guilt. Even as a kid, I knew better than to let my grandmother catch me napping or sleeping in on a Sunday morning. *Nooo*, absolutely not. Growing up, my body just needed more sleep time, so I regularly slept until noon on the weekends and felt guilty for doing so. I would pop my head up like I wasn't sleeping whenever Grandma poked her head into my room. I tried so hard to normalize sleeping in on weekends. But when you come from a family that wakes up at 5:00 a.m. every morning—on purpose—you're fighting a losing battle.

I could not sit idle around the house because Grandma would find something for me to do. Whether it was yard work, cleaning the house, or doing homework, there was always work to be done. If we kids lounged around or played video games for too long, the adults would call us lazy and tell us to find something more "constructive" to do. I still remember the look of disgust in Grandma's eyes whenever I woke up from a midday nap or slept past the acceptable morning wake-up time. Even as an adult, hearing the word *lazy* makes me cringe. I loathe the word *lazy*. I mean, why do I gotta be lazy? Can't I just be tired?

The truth is, naps are viewed as a luxury in American work cultures; it is considered a privilege to stop and rest. We live in a world where capitalism is king. Working tirelessly and pushing beyond personal limits is rewarded, and *rest*, well let's just say it's a foreign concept to most. This type of thinking is also especially prevalent in the entrepreneurial world. "Hustle hard," "team no sleep," "keep grinding"—all of these terms are rooted in busyness and productivity, but they are the complete antithesis to *real* success in my opinion. We see this kind of I'll-sleep-when-I'm-dead messaging everywhere. It's toxic and extremely harmful to our mental health. Especially as new entrepreneurs, we so badly want our businesses to be successful, and that ambition can lure us into dangerous work habits, like not getting enough sleep, neglecting our health, and pushing ourselves beyond our limits.

Team No Sleep

In the early days of my entrepreneurial journey, I would work twelve- to thirteen-hour days. I was building and growing my business nonstop, so that meant working from six o'clock in the morning into the late evening hours. Especially when I worked a full time job, I would work on my business before heading to the office. Most mornings, I was out of the apartment by 8:00 a.m. and did not come home until about ten o'clock at night—only to get back on my laptop and work a few more hours. I didn't know how to stop. At the time, I thought this is what I needed to do to get my business off the ground.

I didn't take a vacation for four years straight. I didn't know what it was to rest and take breaks from work. If I took time away from my business, I was afraid everything would fall apart. I got impatient when I didn't see immediate progress, so I pushed myself even harder.

Bad idea.

I had myself convinced that if I took a break, it meant that *I didn't want it bad enough.* Can you believe that? Honestly, at the time I was convinced it was true because I heard the sentiment often, frequently from other entrepreneurs, many of whom said it while lounging by their pool or as they were about to board their private jet. My mouth salivated. I wanted that life. But really, I just wanted freedom, and I exhausted myself to get it.

Oftentimes our default mode is to power through. To ignore our body's warning signs when we're pushing beyond the brink and need to slow down. One year, my body made the decision to slow down for me. I began to experience really heavy periods, painful cramping, and a protrusion in my lower belly that grew increasingly bigger. There wasn't a baby in there, so I grew concerned about what could be going on in my body. When I finally went to the doctor, I was told I had several fibroids in varying sizes, one in particular that was as large as a cantaloupe. I needed surgery to have them removed. But the thought of being out of work scared me more than the actual surgery. I was afraid that I would run out of money, that I wouldn't be able to get clients, that I would fall behind in my business while I was in recovery. But I had no choice. I was out of commission for six to eight weeks as my body healed. During that time, I had a lot of time to think. I had no choice but to use that time to actually do what I had been avoiding for so long: rest.

Even now, telling that story brings up hard feelings for me. I hate that my body had to damn near break down in order for me to stop and pay attention. I pushed myself so stubbornly that I did not see the early warning signs.

After that experience, I started thinking differently about my health and overall well-being. I not only had to heal my body but also my mind. I had to determine how to prioritize rest. It was something I knew I *needed* to do, but knowing something and actually doing something about it are two different things.

I started making better choices and heeding the signs when my body needed to rest or take a break. Sometimes, the old ways try to resurface. Even now, when I feel myself pushing, I recognize the telltale signs more readily. I know when I'm heading into dangerous territory when my eyes start to burn because I'm staring at the screen for too long. My shoulders become really tense when I try to jam too many things into my day. I'm not prone to headaches, but when I do get them, I know it's because I'm in stress mode, or it's been too long since I've taken a break.

The Impact of Driving Too Hard

When it comes to stress and its impact on our mental and emotional well-being, Black women are disproportionately affected by higher rates of stroke, high blood pressure, and fibroids. Between inequities surrounding race, gender, health, and other systems of oppression, the level of stressors Black women face are constantly rising every day. Because of this, we process and internalize stress differently than our white peers. When we internalize stress and it goes unprocessed in the body, that energy gets trapped and ultimately weakens the body, making us more susceptible to disease, illnesses, and ailments within the body.

I believe my fibroids were a physical manifestation of years and years of unprocessed stress—both mental and emotional. That energy had nowhere else to go, so it turned into a large mass within my body. Hustling and grinding all hours of the day led me straight to Burnoutville. And it wasn't pretty. I was tired all the time, irritable, and always felt rundown. I lost weight because I wasn't eating enough, and I'm already thin, so that was not a good look for me. I hardly saw my friends. Whenever I did hang out for an event not related to business, I would get anxious. I felt like I was "wasting time" that I could have spent working on my business. I totally bought into the hustle mindset.

Living in New York City will do that to you. "Rise and grind" is the mantra. People come to New York from all over the world to follow their dreams, start a business, and pursue their lifelong careers. Nothing stops here; it's called the city that doesn't sleep for a reason. Even when the night club closes, there's always an after-party somewhere. You can get pizza at 3:00 a.m. anywhere in town. Some offices and coworking spaces stay open around the clock. Trains run all hours of the night. If you want to keep going, there are many systems in place to make sure you never have to stop.

The Time We All Stayed Home

When the pandemic hit in early 2020, everything came to a screeching halt. It was the first time ever that the world could pause and hear itself think. Even the ozone layer cooled off because so many of us vacated the roads, tunnels, and airspace. Virtually everything was shut down and canceled that year.

One of my biggest client contracts was canceled, along with a few other speaking events. Like many of us, I suddenly had a lot of time on my hands. With no office to go into and no subway to take me there, I could finally pause long enough to reevaluate my life and career. It became clear as day, that I was not just physically exhausted, my soul was depleted. Up to that point, I had spent every single day of the last decade pounding the pavement, running all over the city, riding the NYC trains uptown, then back downtown to meetings, attending events, holding client meetings, jam-packed conferences, and meeting for networking lunches with so-and-so. I did this without even thinking, every day, back-to-back, with no breaks in between. The grind had become too much.

The pandemic was the wake-up call we all needed to slow down and take stock of what was important. During that pause, I experienced many moments that confirmed I was done with the grind life. One particular moment stands out. It was still in the pandemic's early days, and I took my first car ride out of Brooklyn to a routine doctor's appointment in Manhattan. I sat in the backseat an Uber with my face mask on, peering out the window as we drove over the Manhattan Bridge.

Manhattan. It would seem that every time I've had a huge realization about my life, I'm peering out of a window overlooking a busy Manhattan scene. The first time was when it hit me that I was ready to leave my corporate job. Now, exactly ten years later, I had reached the limit of the hustle and grind that once upon a time in my life seemed so alluring. Concrete sidewalks represented the miles and miles of steps I had taken, exhausted, wearing my "busy badge," walking amongst crowds of equally exhausted people. The fact that such a state was accepted as the normal grind suddenly seemed mind blowing and foreign to me. I decided right then and there, I wasn't going back to that lifestyle.

Go Lay Down

Tricia Hersey, founder of The Nap Ministry, believes in rest as a form of resistance.[32] She regards naps as more than just naps but a way of slowing down, pushing back on capitalism and grind culture so we can reclaim our time as Black and brown folks.

Our society demands we push ourselves to the brink of burnout

---

32   Tricia Hersey, *Rest is Resistance* (Boston: Little, Brown Spark, October 2022).

and exhaustion all in the name of capitalism and productivity. This brainwashing of having to be bigger, better, faster, harder at any costs, has cost us and has us believing that we are not deserving of rest. This idea of prioritizing rest over running yourself ragged is literally pushing back on the systems that make us feel guilty for slowing down and taking a nap.

I had a manager say to me after calling out sick, "Hurry up and get better okay? There's a lot of work to get done." I left that job three months later.

Reject the "hustle hard" mindset when it comes to entrepreneurship. Building your own business can be extremely exhausting, and because you love what you do, it can be easy to keep working without stopping. But the truth is, we are much better businesswomen when we are centering our health and well-being. We are no good to our clients and community if we are not operating from a place of fullness and strength. We go into self-employment most times to experience expansion, freedom, and flexibility, but the more we neglect self-care, the less we experience what we're searching for. Instead, we end up replicating the very habits that caused us to burn out at our full-time jobs.

I can't stress enough the importance of taking time away to restore and replenish, whether that's closing the laptop at 7:00 p.m., scheduling vacation time, or taking on creative passion projects even if they're not related to your business. These things give you energy, not rob you of it. Rest is key. Make time for it—often.

Studies show that just a ten-minute break can have a profound effect on healing daily work stress. One of my favorite articles of all time was written back in 2007, but its principles still hold true many years later. It's called "Manage Your Energy, Not Your Time" by Tony Schwartz and Catherine McCarthy at the *Harvard Business Review*.[33] It states that as work demands continuously rise, many people respond by doing more to keep up. That inevitably leads to burnout. Energy fuels our capacity

---

[33]   Tony Schwartz and Catherine McCarthy, "Manage Your Energy, Not Your Time," *Harvard Business Review*, October 2007, https://hbr.org/2007/10/manage-your-energy-not-your-time.

to work, and managing our energy—not our time—is the best way to get more done faster and better. They make the point that time is a finite resource, but energy is replenishable. When it comes to the four dimensions of energy—the body, emotions, mind, and spirit—when you focus on each bucket of energy, they can be expanded and renewed. Pretty fascinating!

Give yourself permission to take what you need to restore yourself. Your worth is not based on productivity but solely because you're a divine being deserving of ease and freedom.

Not Returning to Normal

As of this writing, we are still wading through the pandemic's disastrous impact and figuring out what our new normal looks like. The gears have wound back up again as companies call us back to the office and business as usual. Breaking free from the status quo can be extremely difficult. But it is so imperative that we use this time to heal from what we've all been through as a collective. We have faced two pandemics: a health crisis and a national reckoning with racism. The simple question of "How are you?" can no longer be answered with, "I'm fine."

In a session with one of my mentees, we talked about the power of rest. I asked, "How are you doing?"

Before answering, she took a long exhale, looked at me through the screen of our Zoom call, and replied, "Ariane, I'm just tired."

And the truth is, yes, we are all tired. Daily, we are working harder than ever to take care of ourselves, our families, and our loved ones. On top of seeing Black and Brown bodies being killed seemingly every day, racism and white supremacy is exhausting. Our bodies can feel the impact through anxiety, tension, and overwhelm.

It has been a difficult time for us, but if nothing else, moving through a pandemic and the fight towards racial justice has made clear the importance of prioritizing mental health and making time to rest. Rest is, in fact, a form of resistance to the status quo and the key to staying on top of the game.

Tips to Rest & Recover

Give yourself permission to break out of the patterns that keep you in the cycle of grind culture and center ease instead. While it will take way more than a checklist to reclaim rest, here are a few ways we can start:

Take baths. Immersing yourself in a warm soak with essential oils and bath salts is a glorious way to melt tension from the body. Read your favorite book, pour a glass of wine, and light a candle for ambiance. Let yourself soak for up to thirty minutes. You're guaranteed to float out of the bathtub.

Meditate daily. Whether it's a five-minute meditation in the morning or before bed, taking time to center your mind creates the mental space for you to think clearly and be less reactive. Everyone has five minutes in their day; even a little bit of time goes a long way.

Exercise regularly. Working out is a great way to channel and process any stress in the body. You don't have to break a sweat for this to work. You can even take a slow-paced, restorative yoga class. The point is to get your body moving and release any stagnant energy that can be toxic to the body.

Take naps. Give yourself permission to reframe naps; they're no longer something that you have to feel guilty about! Depending upon how much time you have, take a fifteen-minute break or longer during your day to nap. Restore yourself and just let your body rest.

Set your boundaries. Know what your limits are when it comes to work and protect your energy. Prioritize what you need in order to do your best work and fill those needs first. Sometimes this means saying *no*, stepping away from your desk for breaks, or simply logging off work at a set time at the end of the day.

Enforce said boundaries. Sometimes setting boundaries is easy but actually enforcing them can be a whole other thing. If you're also working on being less of a people pleaser, upholding your boundaries to others might be especially difficult. Enlist help with a supportive partner or work with your therapist on this one. Practicing your boundaries can be especially liberating but give yourself grace and patience too.

Slow down. Society teaches us that we have to speed up to increase output and get ahead. While it seems counterintuitive, sometimes *slowing down* can be even more effective. When we slow down, we are less reactive and become more intentional in how we're working, what we're doing, and who we're being.

Take time off. Sis, I'ma just have you go ahead and put that vacation time on the calendar right now.

Purpose to Practice

Use the following journaling prompts to begin reflecting on rest practices and how you can incorporate them as an essential business practice:

What did work look like in your household growing up? For example, did you work on the weekends? Did your parents ever hold two or more jobs? In what ways did you see your parents rest or take breaks?

What would more rest look like in your life and work right now?

What would you need to take off your plate in order to create more space for downtime?

Chapter 9

CATCHING THE SPIRIT

IN MY FAMILY, WE WERE raised to always put God first in everything. I was baptized as a baby and attended Catholic school for a few years when I was around seven or eight. We always said grace around the table before meals and played gospel music at home on Sundays. We weren't strict about religion by any means, but in my family, God certainly was the center in all things.

As I've grown older, I still rely pretty heavily on my faith. I lean on it when it comes to my career and business. Over the years, I've come to believe that, number one, the work we do through our careers or business is oftentimes a calling that God has placed on our hearts to fill a gap that only we can fill. And number two, entrepreneurship is an actual leap of faith. How far you go will depend on how strongly you are driven by your faith. Whether it's faith in God, love, or the Universe, I do believe a higher power is holding all of this together. That same belief has carried me through some pretty tough times in my life and continues to sustain me today.

Anyone who knows me knows that I'm a pretty spiritual, some might say a "woo-woo," kind of person. And it's all true, I'm a big believer in the mysticism of the Universe. You would not be wrong if you guessed that I indulge in tarot cards, burn sage to cleanse a space on occasion, carry around crystals in my pocket for protection, and make wishes whenever I see the numbers *1111* and have a pretty impressive vision board. Oh, and I pray. A lot. If being too woo-woo is wrong, I don't want to be right.

Although I was raised with traditional Christian teachings, my understanding of spirituality and how I connect with God has evolved over time. As I got older into my adulthood, it was important to me to understand the relationship I wanted to have with God, rather than just accept what was taught to me as a kid. I explored different ideas and teachings and chose what felt right. Today, my spiritual practice feels very personal to me.

My spiritual rediscovery was sparked about a year or two into my business when I started practicing yoga. Without knowing too much about the ancient practice of yoga—it's been around for five thousand years—I was open to trying something new. You could say I was searching for deeper meaning in my life. This whole entrepreneur thing was new to me, and I desperately needed to work through the lingering trauma leftover from my corporate life. I wanted to understand more about myself and who I was becoming as I undertook the gargantuan task of building my business.

In my experience, entrepreneurship is one of the most spiritually transformative journeys one can ever take—if you allow it to be. Entrepreneurship is such an unpredictable journey; there's virtually no certainty involved, and you'll have days where the only thing you can do is pray. I believe to my core that a dedicated spiritual practice can keep us grounded through the inevitable ups and downs of business building.

I immediately discovered that I loved yoga, not for the physical benefits of bending my body in all sorts of poses—I've never been terribly flexible—but for the mental clarity and deep connection to my inner self that I couldn't find anywhere else at the time. Whenever I stepped onto the mat, I felt at ease, no matter what was going on in my life. On the mat, I could slow down, hear my own thoughts, and be present in my body. I found deep comfort in that.

Yoga led me down a path of self-exploration, taking on new ideas and challenging old ones. Rediscovering my spiritual practice may have begun with yoga, but it did not end there. When I read the book, *A New Earth* by Eckart Tolle, my mind was literally blown by the idea that *we are not our thoughts*. Up until then, I had never really considered that our thoughts—the ideas, stories, and beliefs we tell ourselves—are constructed by a separate part of ourselves.

You've likely heard the ego used to describe someone with an overly large bravado. But the ego can mean something different, more sinister. The ego is also an internal voice that is determined to imprison us in our comfort zone. It makes us doubt ourselves by spewing incessant negative self-talk.

Learning these new theories about the inner workings of the mind was revolutionary for me. It was the first time I had ever observed the mental chatter of my inner thoughts and self-talk and saw them as separate from myself. This is going to sound completely crazy, but it was like I was meeting myself again for the first time, like a spiritual reckoning that pushed back on who I thought I was and revealed who I truly am. It changed how I saw myself.

Around the same time, I went "natural" and stopped using chemicals in my hair, so I got to know the real texture of my hair for the first time since I was eight or nine years old. I traded in my corporate high heels for black and white Converse sneakers as I peeled back the layers and became more in touch with my quirky, creative, artistic side. I also started meditating daily.

I stopped listening to outside distractions and trying to force things in my business into what I thought it *should* be and started trusting my intuition more. Looking back, it clearly was the start of the healing journey I so desperately needed.

Healing from Harm

Being a Black woman in corporate America is exhausting. According to an article in *The Cut,* "Black women frequently struggle with microaggressions, a lack of opportunities, and the pressure to be constantly 'on.' Throw in long hours, endless Slack messages, and a culture that prioritizes the go, go, go, and burnout becomes an almost unavoidable condition."

Navigating environments where code-switching, hypervisibility, and microaggressions are so prevalent contributes to higher rates of stress and mental health challenges that impact overall wellness. Mysticism and spirituality can be used as recovery tools for us to empower ourselves and heal from a world where we are often devalued and marginalized.

In mainstream media, spirituality is often shared through a lens of white feminism or something akin to an *Eat, Pray, Love* experience. As Black women, our connection to spirit might look a little different. Not only is running off to Bali indefinitely for a spiritual retreat not relatable to the experiences of most Black women, such ideas do more harm than good when it comes to healing trauma. They may feel like an unattainable luxury to many of us. Aunt Bernadene from the block certainly wasn't hopping a flight when things got bad or when she had to "find herself."

When I started practicing yoga, it was rare to find a yoga teacher who was a person of color. But now, communities of color, and particularly communities of Black women, are seeking out and building spaces dedicated to healing racial trauma and embarking on pathways towards greater self-discovery.

Embracing the Woo

One of my favorite books is *The Alchemist* by Paulo Coelho.[34] In this timeless story of a boy's search for purpose and fulfillment, one passage reads, "When you want something, all the universe conspires in helping you to achieve it." It's the very thing that happens when you make the decision to go full force toward your dreams. It's not a coincidence that

---

34   Paulo Coelho, *The Alchemist* (London: Thorsons, 1995), 22.

once you've made the decision to create your dreams, new opportunities supporting those dreams appear out of nowhere. You just happen to meet the exact person who can help you. You stumble upon the exact information you're looking for. All the doors begin to open for you, and you realize there's no such thing as coincidence. The universe responds with synchronous events to support you, and when it does, you know you are in flow. Life no longer seems like an uphill battle.

Embracing the woo is the practice of believing in a higher order of things even when we can't see it. It's knowing that there is divine timing to how and when things unfold—even if it's not as fast as you wish it would be. In the church, we call this faith. When we have a gift, a calling that is meant to be in the world, we have to be open to letting go, so we can let God. We have to release our plans and expectations, our efforts to control the outcome of what *we* think is supposed to be and when it's supposed to happen. It's an act of surrender.

It's not our job to figure out *the how* of making our dreams a reality. Sometimes the universe has a way of giving us exactly what we want and need in a better way than our limited minds can even imagine. Our only job is to keeping showing up every day and staying the course of our dreams. Say yes to what feels right for you, and trust that each step of your path will be revealed in the right time, even if you don't see the whole staircase in front of you.

I see the Universe at work all the time in my work with clients. After a few days of hiring me, one client was let go from her job. While it was devastating news on the surface, it was exactly what was needed to spark the change she sought. She didn't like her job anyway and planned to leave and start her own company, but the Universe made everything happen a little sooner than she expected.

This is how the Universe creates space in our lives—by taking away what no longer serves us so that we can make room for new things to enter. When something is taken away from us, our first reaction is to resist and hold on. Losing something comfortable or familiar to us—even when we know it's not good for us—is like losing a piece of our identity. But oftentimes, we only see a limited version of who we truly are. A higher power sees us as so much more than that—and it helps us see that too.

So many times I lost a big client or a contract and thought it would devastate my business. Many times, I thought for sure, *This is it,* and I would need to close down. But riding through those challenges, I learned to see what I could control, like my reaction and my mindset, and what I couldn't control, like the market, slow seasons, and so on. With those insights, I held on even tighter to my inner faith.

Our thoughts are the most powerful tools we have to build the lives we truly want. Our thoughts quite literally create the reality we experience. Constantly feeding the brain negative thoughts—*It's impossible, it won't work out, there isn't enough money, clients, or time*—creates that reality. The brain takes our thoughts as instructions. It's why at times we self-sabotage when things are actually going well.

Conversely, thoughts of abundance and possibility—despite what things may look like on the outside—direct the brain to create those things in reality. Bell Hooks writes in her book, *Sisters of the Yam*:

> The vast majority of black people, particularly those of us from non-privileged class backgrounds, have developed survival strategies based on imagining the worst and planning how to cope. Since the "worst" rarely happens, there is a sense of relief when we find ourselves able to cope with whatever reality brings and we don't have to confront debilitating disappointment. Certainly choosing to worry as a coping mechanism to ward off possible future discomfort isn't enough of a reason to create that kind of stress in your life. Thinking positively isn't about lying to yourself or being in denial; it's about choosing your own perspective to create the reality we want to live in and how we want to feel.[35]

35   Bell Hooks, *Sisters of the Yam: Black Women and Self-Recovery* (Boston: South End Press, 1993), 46.

When I first moved to the city, I spent a lot of time in Brooklyn. I actually lived in Queens at the time, but just about every weekend I'd drive over the Kosciuszko Bridge into Brooklyn to hang out. There was something about the borough's charm that had me hooked. I loved walking past the beautiful brownstones, cozy cafes, and parks; I just fell in love with its vibe. I always thought, *I could live here.* But as much as I relished the dream of living in a cute little Brooklyn neighborhood, actually making that happen felt too far out of reach for me.

Fast forward a few years, and I was in a desperate search for a new apartment. It was at that particularly rough time in my life when I hit financial rock bottom and had to sell all of my belongings after a breakup. After crashing on one too many friends' couches, I needed a new place to live. I gave myself two months to do it.

Now, if you've ever had to apartment search in New York City, you know how absolutely grueling it can be. After poring through countless apartment listings, setting up appointments to view them, chugging on the train to go see as many as ten apartments in one day, I was worn out. Nearly two months later, I still hadn't found a place.

Just when I was about to give up, I checked my inbox to see that one person had responded to my email about an apartment I was interested in. The actual location of the apartment—Brooklyn—didn't even click in my mind at the time. All I knew is that I was desperate to find something. I rode the train from the South Bronx, where I was staying, all the way to downtown Brooklyn. As I made my way to the apartment address, I slowly realized that it was the exact neighborhood I used to come to and dream about living in. I walked through the front door of the apartment and heard a little inner voice whisper, "This is the last apartment you'll have to see for awhile."

It was everything I wanted, right in the heart of a beautiful, vibrant Brooklyn neighborhood. The next day, I received the call: I got the apartment.

This is how living a faith-based life works. Ninety-nine percent of the effort is believing in something we can't always see. We don't need to see gravity to know it exists. We know that electricity is real, even though it isn't visible. We govern our lives based on this knowledge, yet we stop short of believing that maybe, just maybe, there is an invisible force guiding all of it.

Sometimes, our resistance to believing comes from a suspicion that it might actually be true. Think about it. How does an acorn actually grow into an oak tree? How does a person's body just know what to do when they are pregnant? Of course science gives us hard core facts, but we also experience miracles or unexplainable events that happen every day. I believe a divine intelligence has this whole thing figured out, and it does not need any input or interference from us.

While divine intelligence doesn't need anything from us, we still interact with it—especially when it comes to our dreams. No two persons dream alike, and that is what makes yours so special. Your dream belongs to you and only you, and mine belongs to me. That's why we light up when we talk about our dreams. We're excited at the thought of something so uniquely *us*. Talking about them allows us to articulate our vision for the future and how we imagine fulfilling it.

When we feel a yearning, a desire in our hearts, it just doesn't appear out of nowhere. I believe it is *placed* there. I believe the spirit talks to us through our dreams, passions, and desires. When we feel inspired or lit up by an idea, it's our inner spirit's way of letting us know we're on the right track. We spot this when we're in flow, during those moments when we're so deeply engaged in an activity that we lose all track of time. That's when we're in the zone and nothing else matters.

Flow is clearly visible with dancers as they perform. An almost ethereal-like energy takes over. As their bodies moves seamlessly, they aren't dwelling in their heads or thinking about the next move. They are just in the moment, and through pure, raw self-expression, allowing themselves to be moved by a higher power. It's not unlike catching the Holy Spirit at church. When we allow the spirit to enter us and are willing to be led by that energy, we are no longer stuck in our heads but surrendering to a higher intelligence that transcends the mind.

Sometimes when I get quiet and clear out the distractions, I can hear the voice of spirit guiding me. When I deeply connect with my inner spirit through meditation, I experience some of the most profound moments.

One evening, during an especially rocky time in my business, while sitting in complete silence, I asked, "What do I need to do to grow my business?"

At first, I heard nothing, but I stuck with it and quietly listened. Then a still, calm voice spoke as clear as day: "Stop hiding."

Immediately, ease flooded my body, relief followed by a rush of emotion. It was true. I was hiding in my business, and my spirit gently reflected that back to me. I had zero doubt that what I had experienced was the guidance of a higher power. All I had to do was open myself up to receive it.

The Mind-Spirit Connection

I had another profound spiritual experience I won't forget. One day during a client session, I sat in a conference room across from a woman I had recently started working with. She began telling me how she dreamed of creating her own line of artisanal spices and selling them in marketplaces worldwide.

As I listened to her, a small voice whispered, "She lost a child."

The words were as clear as day, yet the voice did not come from my client. It came from inside of *me*. I realized it was my intuition speaking. But that wasn't the freakiest part. Almost immediately after I heard those words, my client, who had been talking the whole time, said to me, "This year, my husband and I lost a child, and we have been dealing with a lot."

I nearly fell off of my chair. How was it possible that I knew this woman had lost a child *before* she had actually told me?

I could have chalked up what happened that day as some coincidence that had nothing to do with anything, or I could pay attention to what I had experienced and explore it. That evening, after meeting with my client, I ran to the nearest bookstore and bought a copy of *Intuition for Beginners* to start honing my intuition.[36] What I experienced that day was undeniable. I believed it helped me, so rather than ignore it, I wanted to understand how to tap into it.

Though we might not realize it, every one of us is intuitive. We each have a deeper knowing about things that goes beyond logic and our analytical minds. Intuition is knowing something without being sure *how* you know it. You just do. Intuition comes to us in a variety of ways, but most commonly through sensation in our stomachs—what we often call a gut feeling—or, as I experienced, through an inner voice. Science actually proves this through the vagus nerve. A *Psychology Today* article states that "Your vagus nerve is constantly sending updated sensory information about the state of your body's organs, digestive track, heart rate, etc. 'upstream' to your brain via different nerves. Eighty to 90 percent of the nerve fibers in the vagus nerve are dedicated to communicating the state of your viscera to your brain in the form of gut feelings."[37]

I mean, need I say more? We have an actual information hub centered within our body that readily delivers essential information to help us navigate decisions.

Our intuition represents our highest, wisest selves. It is an inner source of information that serves as a GPS for decision making about people, situations, leading, and living. But how do you know when you're hearing the voice of intuition? In my experience, the intuitive voice doesn't try to convince or influence; it just provides information that you can either take or leave. When I hear my intuitive voice, I can only describe it as something that cuts through noisy mental chatter with minimal effort. It's a distinct voice that doesn't sound like the usual, anxious sounding, always processing, overly analyzing, self. No. The

---

36   Diane Brandon, *Intuition for Beginners (Woodbury: Llewellyn Publications, 2013).*

37   Christopher Bergland, "Trust Your Gut—There's Nothing Woo-Woo About the Vagus Nerve," *Psychology Today, September 23, 2016,* https://www.psychologytoday. com/ca/blog/the-athletes-way/201609/trust-your-gut-theres-nothing-woo-woo-about-the-vagus-nerve.

intuitive voice sounds calm, confident, and doubt free. And I access her (yes, my intuitive voice is a she) by slowing down and listening within.

More times than not, however, we do not trust the voice of our intuition. Sometimes, trauma and unprocessed emotional pain can actually cut us off from that inner voice. We have been conditioned to doubt, deny, and distrust anything that cannot be proven or measured with logic.

The intuitive voice is anything but logical and linear. Intuition doesn't usually come with a set of facts or evidence about why we should move across the country or take that new job even when it means taking a pay cut. We're accustomed to needing clear, logical reasons *why* we should trust what the inner wisdom is telling us. That often leads us to ask other people what we should do or research answers incessantly, even when the right answer is already in front of us. And that's ok. Sometimes gathering information before coming to a conclusion is part of our decision-making process. If so, we should honor that. We just have to be careful not to get so swept up in seeking external answers that it drowns out our own inner knowing.

Intuition is the secret weapon of most entrepreneurs. Honing and developing it can mean all the difference in how effective and successful we are as leaders.

Accessing Your Intuition

Learning to trust your instincts is a practice. The ability to hear your intuitive voice takes time and patience. You can't just go from ignoring intuition for years to suddenly starting to hear it today. Unfortunately, it doesn't work that way. Think of it like this: Imagine you have a friend who thinks highly of you, always offers the best advice and guidance, is your companion, and is there for you wherever you go. Say you haven't been treating this friend very well. You don't listen to her advice, you tell her to be quiet, and you question her all the time. After a while, this friend will take the hint and go silent. If you turn around after years of ignoring her and suddenly want to be close again, this friend might need some time to come around. So it goes with the intuitive self.

To rekindle this very sacred relationship to your inner knowing, you must learn how to quiet your mind. Spend time alone with yourself. Break away from the noise and distractions around you and go within through practices like meditation and journaling.

When I started my business journey, I had to relearn how to lean on intuition to help me make the best decisions and navigate one of the scariest paths I had ever embarked on. I had to unlearn the habit of listening to other people's opinions and start listening to myself again. Reconnecting with my intuition was like coming home to myself, discovering a new part of me that had been dormant. Healing inner challenges and emotional blocks came from confronting them through raising my self-awareness and learning to trust how to listen to my own needs again. Working with a therapist also helped tremendously.

I picked up a book called *The Artist's Way* by Julia Cameron many years ago, and this book led me to begin a journaling practice called, *morning pages*.[38] Morning pages is the practice of filling up three pages of my journal with any thoughts and feelings first thing in the morning. At first, rolling out of bed to journal felt stumbly and pointless, but I stuck with it. Some days it seemed as though I had nothing to say, and other times, the words just poured out of me. It was the first time I'd listened to my own voice to hear what it had to say. Most days, my writing was always me worrying about something. I wrote a lot about my fears too. Looking back on some of my older journals, I can always tell the place I was in emotionally by the things I had written about. It's kinda nice seeing my growth and progression over the years too, and noting challenging times I had overcome. Writing my thoughts down every day gave me space to put my feelings on paper, and soon it became something I looked forward to. Coming to the page became a soothing release for me.

Over time, I noticed a new voice emerged from those pages; a voice

---

38   *The Artist's Way: A Spiritual Path to Higher Creativity*. New York, NY, G.P. Putnam's Sons, 1992

that was different than the mental chatter I was used to hearing. I began finding clarity through my writing. Journaling became my problem solver, leading me through difficult decisions and emotional blocks. Writing became one of the mediums of connecting to my intuitive voice. On my worst days and through my biggest decisions, writing invariably brings me to a place of understanding, peace, and clarity about what to do next. Sometimes it takes a while to reach clarity, but the practice has never steered me wrong.

The Intersection of Business and Spirituality

Spirituality in business is often considered taboo, but studies have shown that people who are driven by their values and a compassion-first approach find greater fulfillment and deeper satisfaction. Imagine starting work meetings with intention through a moment of silence, or having each person share something they're grateful for, or expressing appreciation. This helps ground people and shift them into a positive mindset for a productive discussion. How refreshing would that be for your team to reduce burnout and enhance collegial connection? In one of my previous roles, my team and I would start off our weekly meeting with a round of "kudos," where we'd take turns sharing something that we admired about each person on our team or shout them out for a job well done. Sometimes I found it kind of hokey, but it certainly helped lift the energy before diving into the rest of the business agenda items.

Imagine giving intuition a seat at the table when making business decisions instead of relying on data and logic alone. Imagine that a sense of purpose and deeply held compassion for others took precedence over profits and quarterly earnings. Practices of prayer, moments of silence, visioning, and rounds of deep, centered breathing can mean all the difference in how well we lead and how connected we feel.

By interviewing and studying the work of hundreds of successful women in business, I found one common theme greatly influenced their success: *They each considered themselves spiritual thinkers.* Whether they believed in God or practiced Buddhism or Kabbalah or ancient indigenous mystical traditions, they had a connection to a higher power that supported and guided them at work and not just on Sundays. Their faith was key to elevating their confidence, providing certainty, and arming them with the ability to weather the ups and downs facing all businesses. Being grounded in the face of adversity, challenges, and uncertainty comes from a strong, spiritual foundation that gives rise to a strong sense of Self.

Spirituality in business culture has not been traditionally accepted. It goes against everything we've ever been taught about business. Wall Street was literally built on greed, aggression, and control, demanding you be a pushy control freak to achieve success at all costs. Always look like you're in control or risk being perceived as weak or passive.

But releasing the need to control and the pressure to achieve is anything but passive; it's the most powerful thing we can do. Releasing expectations and our own assumptions creates breathing room and allows something greater than we've ever imagined to come forward. This is the battle between the mind, which always seeks control and safety, and the heart, which laughs in the face of logic. Many of us spend too much time in our own heads. Constantly analyzing, calculating, and clinging to logic has made us forget how to leave room for creativity and imagination. Playing the worst case scenario over and over in our heads crushes creativity. We need both the heart and the mind to align as dreamer and project manager, respectively.

Spirituality can show up in many ways in your business: balancing logic-based decisions with intuitive ones, meditating before attending a meeting or high stakes interaction, stating words of affirmation throughout the day, praying before the day begins, or practicing gratitude at the end of a work week.

One of my favorite spiritual practices is starting my day with a mantra before I get out of bed in the morning: "Bless this day ahead." No matter what the day brings, I proactively throw good vibes out there before the day has even begun.

In another practice, whenever I send out a new client proposal, or I am about to do something huge in my business, I say softly out loud, "Let the highest outcome be had." This way I know that whatever happens, even if the answer is *no*, it will be for the highest good. I can let go of any pressure or expectation for the outcome. It helps me relax and reminds me that a greater power is in control.

The way to align is through practices that quiet the mind and shift you into a focus of positivity and joy. Some of my favorite grounding practices that can be used at work are:

- Meditating for five minutes every morning before starting your day
- Starting or ending your day with a gratitude practice
- Journaling and writing out your innermost thoughts
- Practicing the power of pause or taking a breath before reacting to any stressful situation
- Visualization and seeing the desired reality you want to create
- Practicing compassion and treating yourself as you would a dear loved one
- Praying or saying words of affirmation

And now I'll do you one better. For fun, I also tune into the phases of the moon to guide my business. Stay with me now . . .

Fun fact: The New Moon represents the start of a new lunar cycle and can be used to symbolize new beginnings. On the first day of the New Moon, the moon is at its darkest point in the sky. As the days pass, it gradually begins to illuminate from the light of the sun. The energy of this phase marks a good time to work on new projects or aim for new goals. On the other hand, the culmination of the Full Moon is a good time to slow down, process, and reflect.

These phases repeat themselves over and over again each month. I like to pay attention to what phase the moon is in to help me know the best time to start something new or when to slow down and be still. I don't hold myself to any strictness here, but you gotta admit there's something kind of fun and witchy about using the moon's energy as a guide. I told ya, my woo-woo game is on point!

There's something about using the laws of nature and tuning into the rhythm of the universe to make it work for us that feels so empowering. From the cycle of the seasons, the tides of the ocean, the ebbs and flows of nature—everything is interconnected! We can actually tap into the life force of nature and be in its rhythm to experience more alignment within our lives instead of going against the grain. That to me is what it means to be in true flow with life.

Creating Your Own Spiritual Practice

What does it mean to have a spiritual practice? What does it look like for you?

Cultivating a spiritual practice takes time and is deeply, deeply personal. The beautiful thing about is that there are many ways to connect with and deepen your spirituality. There's no "right" way to do it. With intention, anything can become a spiritual experience—like taking a walk or hiking through nature, playing with a dog, looking into the eyes of a newborn baby, going for a run, or sitting quietly by the ocean.

Spirituality practice cultivates greater self-awareness. Through awareness, you become the observer of your thoughts, feelings, and behaviors so that you can choose who you want to be. Notice the places where you are living in autopilot mode and infuse more intention in your choices.

I predict we are at the forefront of a radical change in how we do business. More and more, we crave a deeper sense of purpose through our work and closer connections to each other. As we look for more meaningful pathways of healing, we are redefining our sense of self to be more grounded in truth. We find truth by remembering that we are here on this earth with one life, and that we each get to choose how we spend it. When we are self-aware and living with purpose, the amazement, wonder, and joy we get to experience every moment is far beyond anything we can ever imagine.

Maybe the saying is true. We really could just be spiritual beings having a human experience.

Purpose to Practice

Whether you're new to meditation, a seasoned meditator, or you've tried it one or two times in the past, indulge me for a moment and try an experiment. Commit to seven days of meditation.

Over the next seven days, I want you to meditate for five minutes each morning before you start your day. Spend five minutes in total silence. That's it. Even Beyonce has five minutes in her day, so you can find five minutes to do this practice.

Find a quiet spot in your home or wake up just five minutes earlier before getting out of bed. Sit with your thoughts for ten glorious minutes and focus on your breathing. Set an alarm on your phone. Do this for seven days and journal what you notice.

Chapter 10

THE PATH FORWARD

IF YOU TAKE NOTHING ELSE from this book, know this: You owe it to yourself to go for your dreams. Period. That's the tweet. Queen, you don't have that type of time to waste. There's never been a more perfect moment than *right now* for you to pursue and build the things that matter to you, and to do so without apology.

We are in a new world right now. So much is changing all around us, and there is no going back to the "normalcy" of pre-pandemic days. As I write this, over 6.84 million people have died of COVID worldwide; over a million in the US alone.[39] Why would we want to go back to the status quo, knowing full well we were never happy then? Not to get preachy on y'all right now, but if the pandemic has taught us anything, it's that life can be incredibly unpredictable, and our time on this earth is precious. Why waste another second holding back on living full out?

Mama Oprah has repeatedly expressed the sentiment that behind our biggest fears are our greatest breakthroughs. Read that one more time. Bigger fears mean bigger breakthroughs. Something amazing awaits on the other side.

---

39   WHO Coronavirus (COVID-19) Dashboard, World Health Organization, February 3, 2023. https://covid19.who.int/.

During any time of uncertainty, we can all ask ourselves *What is this experience showing me?* During the pandemic, we saw the harsh realities of the racial discrepancies faced by people of color. Many people reevaluated their values around work and determined they needed better options than what they had, which led to the Great Resignation. Similarly, employers had to reckon with what their employees required to do their best work, and they had to resolve to change antiquated, toxic work cultures to keep people happy. It took the world shutting down to realize these things, but like I shared at the start of this book, pain is the ultimate motivator towards making a change.

You are the missing puzzle piece the world needs right now. Going for your dreams isn't just about you anymore but the people who need what you have to give. Someone is always watching what you do; whether it's your kids or people on social media, you are inspiring someone in some way. You just never know how what you do and who you are can inspire someone to take bold, powerful steps within their own lives. I regularly watch so many all-star, fierce, Black women who are out there doing their thang and inspiring me to reach still higher. I strongly believe that when you go for your dreams, it gives other Black and Brown girls the permission and inspiration to go for theirs. If *she* can do it, *you* can do it. If *you* can do it, *they* can do it.

We need your voice, we need representation, and we need the work that only you can do. We need you to be out there in action kicking ass and taking names so we can see what is possible and change the narrative of who we truly are. The only way this world will change is with each of our unique gifts in play.

Black women are in the fight of their lives right now. Opportunities to meet the moment are endless. Demand is high for the value we alone can bring. I imagine a world where Black women who know what it's like to be on food stamps and raised in public housing go on to become CEOs of their own businesses or Fortune 500 companies. I imagine us building new tables for us to sit at filled with swaths of Black women leaders, change makers, shit stirrers, disrupters, and innovators, all breaking barriers and reclaiming our time. I imagine industries like tech, medicine, engineering, finance, and other underrepresented fields including the voices of Black women who know they belong in the room.

I want to see the *Wall Street Journal*, *Entrepreneur*, and every major publishing outlet regularly featuring women of color of all ages, gender expansive identities and abilities on their covers, raising the visibility of our generation's leaders, and creating a ripple effect to pave the way for up-and-coming generation of leaders. I want to live in a world where *Support Black Businesses* is no longer a hashtag but a normalized way of doing business.

So where do we go from here?

This moment brings an amazing opportunity to chart a new path forward as the answer to our ancestors' wildest dreams. At this lovely intersection of hope and restoration, we can ask ourselves these questions:

What do I want my life and career to look like?

What dreams have I been sitting on for way too long?

What does taking a leap in my work look like to me now?

While having hope can spark limitless possibilities, inspiration, and the courage to persevere, it can easily fizzle out if there is no accompanying action. We must take action—and not just any ol' action. Purposeful, intentional, eye on the prize, and dog-with-a-bone conviction must drive those actions, particularly as it pertains to impacting change through our work. Many of us can say we have taken action throughout our careers, but how much of it was merely checking a box versus acting with purposeful intention in the direction of our dreams? Anything less than purposeful only yields more of the same, business as usual, status quo results.

It's time we start listening to our dreams instead of our fears. It's time for us to start the work—*today*—instead of putting things off until the future. It's time we start trusting in our dreams because without them, life starts to feel pretty empty.

It has been my dream to write this book you're now holding in your hands. I'm here to report that dreams really do come true. I'm living proof. If I, a girl from the Bronx who started a typing business from her dorm room in college can do it, trust me, you certainly can. As long as you're here on this earth, there is still work for you to do. Our work. The choice is yours, right now. This moment is yours, right now. Younger generations will get to walk through the doors you broke down today because you dared to follow your truth.

So. always keep dreaming. On purpose.

Purpose to Practice

To all my Sisters with dreams, take the *Dreaming on Purpose* pledge:

I will always say **yes** to myself and my dreams.

I will take steps to get clear on what I want to achieve, what I want my business to be, and why that is important to me.

I will work to get rid of destructive excuses. I know that they will only slow me down, and I can turn them into creative solutions.

I will learn to take up space and get out of my comfort zone more. I know that doing the things that scares me is the fastest way to grow.

I will stay the course and not be deterred by disappointment or rejection. I know that if I keep going, I will eventually get to where I want to be.

I will envision my success every step of the way and take actions that support my visions.

I will learn from failure and see it as a breakthrough in disguise. I know that it is never personal but always an opportunity to grow and get better.

I will always ask for help when I need it. I know that having an army of angels to support me makes me stronger.

I will be gentle on myself and take care of my needs to avoid burning out. I will practice prioritizing self care and learn to rest more.

I will start from where I am using the resources I have available to me right now, even if it's not much. I know that I have everything I need to get me to the next step.

_____   _____

Signature   *Date*

ABOUT THE AUTHOR

CAREER EQUITY AND WORK CULTURE LEADER, entrepreneur, and keynote speaker Ariane Hunter is a voice for her generation of Black women professionals, women who want to reject the status quo, heal from soul sucking jobs, and center their dreams again. She brings over twenty years of combined career and leadership strategy to help marginalized groups thrive and build healthy relationships with work. Ariane is a mental health advocate for Black women and believes in strong boundaries and restful practices as keys to a thriving work life. Her extensive training is rooted in social justice, technology, intersectionality and futurist insights for sustainable, impactful change.

A New Yorker at heart, Ariane has supported high profile clients to become key players in their industry. She holds an MBA and is a certified coach. Ariane was hand selected for NYC's inaugural BE NYC mentoring program for entrepreneurs, a program that was endorsed by Bill De Blasio. She has worked with industry leaders and brands including Evernote, Hewlett Packard, Oracle, Women in Stem Leadership at Stony Brook University, and many more. She has spoken for The Grio, PepsiCo, Ladies Get Paid, NYU Stern Women in Business, and Advancing Women in Tech. A featured guest on numerous career empowerment podcasts, Ariane is also a published writer whose work appears on Time.com and The Muse. She's been quoted in CNBC, Yahoo News, Business Insider, Girlboss, Diversity Inc, The Daily Worth, Her Agenda, and more.

She lives in Brooklyn with her fiancé and their adorable pup.

ACKNOWLEDGMENTS

TO MY GRANDMA, THE LATE Barbara Naomi Davis, the original dream chaser. Without your courage to take the leap and come to this country, I would not be here. I will always keep dreaming in your honor.

To Mom, who taught me grace, courage, and to always ask for what I want. Through you, I know that all things are possible with faith.

To Dad, who always reminds me to keep my head up and hold my crown. You continue to make me proud to be your daughter.

To my big brother and my forever cheerleader, thank you for always being in my corner and reminding me to always stay true to myself.

To my one and only, thank you for always seeing me and showing me what's possible through a love that knows no bounds. There is no one else I would rather dream on purpose with.

www.ingramcontent.com/pod-product-compliance
Lightning Source LLC
Chambersburg PA
CBHW052042090426
42739CB00010B/2019